OLD TRACTORS

and the Men Who Love Them

Dedicated to the tractor professors,
whose seminars have taught me so much—
Dennis Adams, Mel Grim, Mel Halsey, Don Hochstetler,
Mick Maun, Dale Muhlbach, Kenny Porath,
Mark Sautter, Al Schmitt, Dan Selden, Bud Stoeger,
and my Dad, Chris Welsch.

Pilgrim: But, Master, I am not ready for the world.
You have given me no answers!
Master: Ah, yes, my son, but I have given you the questions.
—George Schwelle, *Visions*

OLD
TRACTORS
and the Men Who Love Them

**How to Keep Your Tractors Happy
and Your Family Running**

Roger Welsch

Motorbooks International
Publishers & Wholesalers ®

First published in 1995 by Motorbooks International Publishers & Wholesalers, PO Box 2, 729 Prospect Avenue, Osceola, WI 54020 USA

Motorbooks International is a certified trademark, registered with the United States Patent Office

The information in this book is true and complete to the best of our knowledge. All recommendations are made without any guarantee on the part of the author or Publisher, who also disclaim any liability incurred in connection with the use of this data or specific details

We recognize that some words, model names and designations, for example, mentioned herein are the property of the trademark holder. We use them for identification purposes only. This is not an official publication

Motorbooks International books are also available at discounts in bulk quantity for industrial or sales-promotional use. For details write to Special Sales Manager at the Publisher's address

Library of Congress Cataloging-in-Publication Data
Welsch, Roger L.
    Old tractors and the men who love them/Roger Welsch.
        p. cm
    Includes index.
    ISBN 0-7603-0129-8
    1. Farm tractors—Conservation and restoration. I. Title.
TL233.25W45   1995
629.225—dc20   95-389

On the front cover: Roger (left) and Sweet Allis, his beloved Allis Chalmers WC, basking happily in the Nebraska sunshine on the Welsch tree farm near Dannebrog. *Lee Klancher*

On the title page: Painting inspired by an old tractor found alongside the road (and an old tractor restorer found in comparable condition at the University of Nebraska). *Linda Welsch*

On the back cover: Corn field backdrop. *Randy Leffingwell*

Printed and bound in the United States of America

Contents

Acknowledgments

◆

I am grateful to Dave Mowitz, machinery editor, and to *Successful Farming* magazine, Dave Howe, editor, and *Nebraska Farmer* magazine, and Linda Tank, editor, Vittorio Maestro, editor, and *Natural History* magazine, and *Cenex Land o' Lakes Cooperative Partners* magazine for permission to reprint my articles previously printed in their pages. Writers always use lines like "this book would not have been possible without..." and I suppose it's often true, but it is never more true than as I write this now: This book would not have been possible without the kindness, generosity, and alertness of Steve Johnson.

Steve, a NASA employee, watches CBS's "Sunday Morning," and took the time and trouble to write that he likes my essays on that program. And he sent along some NASA materials for my astro-nut daughter, Antonia. And Antonia wrote him, and he wrote us. Then, one day when he was cruising the Internet, whatever that means, he saw a note from Lee Klancher that Motorbooks International was looking for someone who might be interested in writing a tractor book. Steve contacted Lee and me and Lee and I got together, and this book is the result. I think of this opportunity as a gift from God, but for the moment, I'll thank Steve Johnson...without whom this book would not have been possible.

I understand that sometimes product names that are specific trademarks creep into common usage without the proper capitalization or that annoying little "®". I use Craftsman®, Coca-Cola®, EZ-Out®, Form-A-Gasket®, JB Weld®, Kroil®, Lime-Away®, Liquid Wrench®, Mack®, Malco®, Mystery Oil®, Snap-On®, Snap-Up®, Sheetrock®, Stanley®, Visegrip®, WD-40®, Xerox®, and undoubtedly a few others throughout the book and hereby announce that I recognize that they are registered trademarks and blah, blah, blah. Frankly, I've always considered the whole concept of trademarks to be a remarkably flattering process, but you know how fussy lawyers can be. I look forward to the day when attractive young ladies ogle some stud and say, "Wow, Heather, look at that hunk o' muscle. He's a real roger, isn't he?" But never mind: I use these names with only the most positive of intentions.

As always, I am deeply indebted to my wife, partner, illustrator, and friend Linda for her patience, talent, and encouragement; I can't imagine working on tractors without her. Or living in this world without her, for that matter.

Introduction

◆

"*O*kay, so I don't know many of the answers," I explained to the publisher of this volume. "Thing is, most books like this are written by experts who have forgotten the kinds of problems beginners like me run into. I'm a beginner, nothing but a raving, innocent enthusiast in tractor rebuilding. I haven't even gotten to restoration. But, believe me, I know all the questions!" And I guess he bought the idea, because here I am.

Telling my mechanic, machinist, welder, and farmer friends I was about to do a book on rebuilding tractors was a little tougher. "Most people wait to write a book until they know everything there is to know about some subject," I said. "But by then their heads are so cluttered with information, they can't figure out what to put in and what to leave out. Me, I figure anyone can write about what they know a lot about. It takes a really smart guy to write a book about something he knows next to nothing about." They nodded, agreeing pretty much that when it comes to restoring old tractors, I know next to nothing, all right. In fact, up until four years ago I hadn't so much as changed the oil in an automobile, and I was 54 years old. It's true. For thirty years I taught languages,

literature, and folklore at Nebraska colleges and finally the University of Nebraska. I wrote books about folklore theory, folk arts, and folk tales. Thoughts of oily engines, greasy transmissions, dented sheet metal, stuck bolts never—NEVER—crossed my mind. I almost bragged, "All I know about motor vehicles is—water in the front, gas in the back, key in the middle, money all over."

Then something happened that changed my life in many ways, all for the better. I fell in love. With a tractor. A battered 1937 Allis Chalmers WC. And it was one of those wonderful romance stories where a male clod pals around with a faithful and adoring but sort of plain girl, and almost too late (but just in time) figures out that she is actually the dame he's been looking for all his miserable life, and, now that he thinks about it, is actually downright pretty.

In December 1974, exactly twenty years and one day ago from the moment I am writing these words, I bought a piece of overgrazed, cactus-infested pasture land on the Middle Loup River near Dannebrog, Nebraska. The next year, in keeping with my hopeless, lifelong preoccupation with salvage, I rescued an 1872 log house that was about to be pushed over and burned and moved it out to a grove of huge, old cottonwoods on my new land, where friends helped me rebuild it.

One of those friends was Dave Ratliff, who looked around the wasteland I was calling a farm and said, "Well, this isn't much of a farm if you don't have a tractor, Rog." He said he had an old Allis Chalmers he hadn't used for a few years, sitting in a weed patch out behind another friend's farmstead. If I wanted it, he said, I could go get it. I called a colleague at the University, Gene Harding, who had a trailer and we went to look at this alleged tractor.

There it sat—orange, rusty, battered, buried in weeds—just the sort of thing you'd expect by way of a freebie tractor. I'll admit, it was not an encouraging sight. We put the trailer in position to winch the battered machine up onto the bed, and Gene said, "Hand winching this wreck up is going to be a real job. Why don't we slosh a cup or two of gas in it and see if it'll start?"

I presumed he was crazy. There was no way this pile of scrap iron was going to start. But we put some gas in it, hooked a chain from the tractor to the pickup, and I climbed into the iron seat—the first moment I had sat behind a tractor's steering wheel in my entire life. Gene pulled me forward about six feet and I released what I presumed was the clutch. There were a couple tentative pops, a shower of mouse nests, dirt, smoke, wasp nests, and weed seeds—and Sweet Allis, as she was almost instantly dubbed, roared to life—just as she would do without fail forever from that moment on for the next twenty years, until right now.

I drove Sweet Allis onto the trailer, Gene laughing at the stupid grin on my face. I should have sensed my fate from that very moment...but I didn't. You know how men are about romance and girls who seem plain to begin with but over time get downright pretty.

For the next fifteen years Sweet Allis sat outside at my farm, covered only by a tarp. In sub-zero weather, untouched for two months, when no other vehicles would run, Sweet Allis never failed me. I always knew I could pull off the tarp and turn her crank, and she would start. And she always did.

I used Sweet Allis to pull a single-bottom plow to plant trees (my place is a certified tree farm), haul logs, plow snow from the road, pull hay racks and toboggans on New Year's Eve, drive to town on sunny days, and haul garbage. I liked the tractor, and recognized and admired its faithfulness. I bragged about its reliability and sturdiness. However, when old farmer friends would ask, "Is your Allis a WC or a C or WF or what?" I'd have to confess, "Beats me. All I know is she's an Allis because that's what it says on the radiator." Every couple years when I figured she needed an oil change or lube job, I took her to the filling station in town, which no self-respecting farmer would ever do, but mechanicking, even to the sub minimal degree of basic maintenance, was simply not for me.

In addition to writing for newspapers, magazines, and books, about eight years ago I began writing scripts for a segment of CBS's show "Sunday Morning with [at that time] Charles Kuralt." We were shooting a piece on the role of farm dogs and we went a few miles west of my place to visit Johnny Fanta, because he had a dog with a reputation for being the meanest mutt around. And we needed a mean dog. Well, Johnny's dog was pretty mean, all right, but while we were shooting, I noticed off in some trees and weeds, there sat a tractor, almost exactly like mine. I braved the nasty dog and waded through the weeds. Sure enough, it was an Allis just like Sweet Allis, same model and everything, whatever that was.

As we left Johnny's place, I remarked off-hand—who knows why?—"Hey, Johnny, if you're ever interested in getting rid of that old Allis rusting back in your woodlot, give me a call." I forgot about the remark, and I presumed Johnny did too, since I didn't hear anything from him. But then one day a couple years later he did call; he said he was cleaning up the wood lot and was interested in getting rid of the old Allis. He even had a front-end dolly I could use to haul the old girl home.

As fate would have it, the friend who went with me over to Johnny's to get the tractor (and fend off that same mean ol' dog) was Dave Ratliff, the same guy who gave me Sweet Allis. We had to cut some trees out from this Allis (which came to be known as the Fantasizer, with a lot more meaning than I knew at the moment) and used a come-along to winch the tractor's front wheels into Johnny's dolly, but we got the job done and hauled the tractor the short five miles to my place. I still had no idea what I was going to do with it, no idea why I had bought it. The spare parts it could provide meant nothing to me since I did no repair on the tractor I had; spare parts were scarcely a priority. My fate was as dim at that moment as it had been fifteen years before.

We jockeyed the tractor into a place where I figured I could park it, for whatever reason. We got out of my pickup and rolled the Allis back out of the dolly. We were about to drive the dolly back to Johnny's when Dave once again uttered the fateful words: "Why don't we slosh a cup or two of gas in it and see if she'll start?"

I presumed he was crazy. There was no way this tractor was going to start. But we put some gas in it, hooked a chain from the tractor to the pickup, and I climbed into the iron seat—the second tractor's steering wheel I sat behind in my entire life. Dave pulled me forward about six feet and I released the clutch. There were a couple tentative pops, a shower of mouse nests, dirt, smoke, wasp nests, and weed seeds—and the Fantasizer roared to life—just as she would do without fail forever from that moment on.

I went to bed that night a different man, but not as different as I would be only a month later.

Later, I lay in bed, wondering about the two old Allises sitting in the yard. How many millions (billions? trillions?) of times had their pistons gone up and down in their hard-working lives? How long had they sat neglected in the rain, snow, and dirt? What sort of tenacity could possibly explain their insistence on running? What happened to everything I thought I knew about the delicacy of engines, the fragility of carburetors, the tenderness of electrical systems and tuning, and fuels, and transmissions, and spark plugs, and rods, and pistons, and rings, and all those mysterious mechanisms I had heard about for a half century but never seen? These old tractors seem determined to run on well beyond the limits of steel, copper, and rubber. Could it be that there is more to these old hunks of iron than iron? Do they have a...gulp...soul?

Sometime later that week, I decided maybe I should look the Fantasizer over more carefully. I had just come off a grueling book tour and a harrowing week with my CBS crew. I was worn out, not so much from work as from frustration. My blood pressure was dangerously high, a problem that had been worsening over the past few years. Maybe, I thought, tinkering around with a couple no-brain chores on that tractor would help me relax and sleep a night through for the first time in months.

I cleared weeds and sticks from the Fantasizer's radiator and frame. I pulled out the dipstick—about the only thing I knew how to do on an engine; the oil was filthy. Even a doofus like me could tell that. Okay, it was a nice spring day, so maybe I'd just drain the oil and replace it. And maybe the oil filter. I could do that.

If you have ever looked under a car hood, you'll understand my situation. I drive a 1991 Ford Taurus. Under the hood I can find the radiator cap and the place where you put windshield washer fluid but I cannot for the life of me find the dipstick. Locating spark plugs and oil filter, if the engine has spark plugs and oil filter, is out of the question. No sign of anything recognizable in the tangle of wires, tubes, rods, and hoses.

But on this Allis, there everything is. As I would realize later, an Allis WC has exactly four wires—one to each spark plug, and there are the spark plugs, sitting right out there in sight, unembarrassed, unashamed. You don't even have to lean over to reach the oil filter; it's at waist level, right where any sensible person would expect and want it to be. The oil pan drain plug is no mystery at all, and you don't need a hoist or jack to get under it. A short person can darn near walk under the thing, it sits so high off the ground!

"Wow," I thought. "This isn't going to be so tough." I managed to find a crescent wrench somewhere—I didn't even have a toolbox—and crawled under the engine. I tightened down the wrench and gave a tentative tug at the drain plug. Hmmm. I pulled a little harder. Nothing. I found an old pair of broken visegrip pliers, tightened them down on the plug and gave it another tug. Didn't budge. I pulled harder. Wham, the pliers slipped off and in the process rounded the corners on the plug. Jeez, this is precisely the reason I hate working on cars—it's dirty, sweaty, frustrating business. And I'd managed to bang my knuckles so now blood was mixing in with the dirt and oil. God, I hate this, I said to myself.

I realized that if I used any more force, I was going to twist off the plug or round the corners even worse. I found a rusty file I kept in my chainsaw bucket and touched up the squaring on the plug so I could get a better grip. This time I was even more cautious. Nothing moved and it was clear that I was not going to break that oil plug loose. "Just as I thought," I grumbled. "Mechanicking is not for me. I should have taken the blasted tractor up to Mel at the town service station in the first place."

So I went up to Mel in the second place. "Got any recommendations on how to get a stuck oil pan drain plug loose?" I asked.

"Did you try Liquid Wrench?" he asked.

"Uh, Liquid Wrench?"

"Yeah, here, take this back with you." He handed me a partially filled can of Wrench. "Put plenty of this on the plug, tap it firmly with a hammer a couple times, and try it again tomorrow. If that doesn't work, put more Wrench on it and tap it some more for a couple days. Good luck."

"Yeah, right. Thanks, Mel. I'll need luck."

I did exactly what Mel told me, not at all optimistic, increasingly grumpy about this whole process. And then the fourth day, as if by magic, the plug turned in its threads, first tightly, then smoothly. I drained the dirty oil, replaced the plug, refilled the crankcase with clean oil, and felt as if I had conquered Mt. Everest. Yeah, I know it's goofy, but that's the way it was.

And it wasn't just that I had gotten the plug out and clean oil in. I couldn't help but wonder what this Old Girl thought about being revived and pampered again after all those years of abuse and abandonment. I wondered what the Fantasizer was feeling, with new, clean oil resting in her battered, old crankcase. Right, iron doesn't think or feel anything. Tell that to a sailor about his ship.

When Dave and I picked the tractor up, Johnny Fanta had said something about the left brake not working and tossed a box of strange looking parts into our truck as we left. I looked the parts over. Not a clue. On the other hand, as is the case with the oil filter and pan drain plug, it's not hard to figure out where the brakes are on an Allis WC, or to see how to get at them. There are two big levers right above the rear axle on each side of the seat; a prominent cast-iron cap is fastened to the body on each side with two large bolts. Voila, the brakes.

I used my only crescent wrench (there should be an ASPCOT—American Society for the Prevention of Cruelty to Old Tractors) to turn off the bolts on the right side brake cover and pulled it off to see what an Allis WC brake mechanism is supposed to look like. I cleared away a couple wasp nests and a wad of spider webs. Wow. For me, it was like being the first man at the North Pole. Had anyone ever been in here before? I was amazed. I laughed.

One of the brakes on Sweet Allis had needed adjusting for fifteen years because it pulled back too far for the lock wedge to stay in place but it had never occurred to me to try to understand the complexities of a tractor brake! Man, working on tractor brakes has to be right up there with quantum physics or programming a VCR! But here it was—a simple band around a drum, pulled tight by the most primitive kind of cam setup. One bolt, one spring, a lock nut. That's all there is!

Good grief, knowing as little as I do, even I could figure this out! The adjustment bolt sat atop the brake mechanism as obvious as a sumo wrestler on a burro. I pulled the cotter pin from the screw and tightened it up. Just like that. I opened the brake cap on the left side. Sure. There it was. I looked in the box of parts and there was the missing brake band. The band goes around the drum like this, the pin goes through here, the lock nut here, tighten her up, check to see that the handle is about in the right position when the brake is set, insert a piece of baling wire in the absence of a cotter pin, and...well, I'll be damned! I just fixed a tractor brake!

I finished my work about supper time and went in to clean up. "You're a mess," Lovely Linda said, and she was right. "Yeah, but I feel absolutely great," I laughed. "Best I've felt in a long time."

I went to bed that night, still feeling...well, downright smug about my little mechanical victories. I took my blood pressure. Whoa! What's this? Not just "normal." Below normal. That night I slept the Sleep of the Innocent (and, as I would soon learn, the Sleep of the Tractor Mechanic).

As I went about the next day's chores, I tried to analyze what had happened to me the day before. What was this warm, fuzzy feeling in my gut? I was like a high school boy in love. Why did someone who so thoroughly hated cars and automotive repair suddenly find working on a tractor such a comfort and joy? Maybe I'd inhaled too many fumes from the Liquid Wrench.

And I've been pondering that same thing the past five years since I extracted that stuck drain plug and put back that brake shoe, and here's where I am at the moment: tractor restoration has given my life great comfort and, quite seriously, in my opinion added many years to my life, because:

1) I like problem solving, but not where the problems bear directly on the most important processes of my life;

2) Salvage is in my blood.

I wouldn't dream of building my own house. Too much rides on it. The welfare of my family and possessions depends on strong walls and a tight roof. Actually, it's a matter of life and death. I don't know enough about house construction to risk my life and property on it. On the other hand, the most fun I had in my life up until I discovered tractors (and excluding our honeymoon, of course) was the summer and fall in 1975 when my friends and I rebuilt that old log house down by the river. It didn't matter that the walls weren't square or plumb. If a nail bent over or a board wasn't cut straight, it really didn't matter. Every time we solved another problem, cleared another hurdle, it was an unmitigated victory, unaffected by the fact that our carpentry lacked finesse, in a big way.

What had happened if I had broken off the plug in the Fantasizer's oil pan or been utterly baffled by its defective brake system? Nothing. What would happen if I broke off a pan bolt or ignored a faulty brake on my Taurus? We'd die or lose an awful lot of money we don't have to lose. In other words, when I work with a tractor, there are no losses, only victories. Okay, they're little victories, but these days, in this world, little victories are about all we can ask for.

My relatives on my mother's side were garbage haulers and that's what I wanted to be when I grew up, as I once told our minister to my mother's eternal embarrassment. Not only can I not bring myself to throw anything away, I absolutely rejoice in taking something that has been discarded, given up for lost, and figuring out how to put it back to use—this piece of garbage pasture I have converted into a tree farm, or the abandoned farm house we bought for $350, moved to our farm, and rebuilt, for example, traditional culture reintroduced to contemporary life (remember, my training is as a folklorist!), that sort of thing. What greater pleasure then for this old salvager than to retrieve an abandoned, cold piece of rusted iron from a weed patch and bring it back to life, to hear the engine roar for the first time in years, to feel the warmth from her loyal heart?

In my hopeless love affair with working on old tractors, there's also the matter of my shop. For one thing, there's no telephone in my shop, and that sure makes my time there more pleasant. My shop is quiet, except for the music I enjoy. Linda tells me it smells pretty bad, but to me it's like perfume. I whistle and sing out there, get sweaty and dirty, and enjoy my tools and my tractors. I once addressed The Gathering of the Orange, the annual meeting of Allis Chalmers nuts, and I referred to this obsession of mine as an addiction. There was some complaint about my choice of words, but I think I was right (which may be why there was so much complaint). In these short five years I have gone from thinking of my tractor work as an occasional respite from my work of making a living to considering my work of making a living a petty annoyance that tends to get in the way of the far more important process of working on tractors in my shop.

Fair warning: look out. The same thing could happen to you.

I have continued to increase my time working with my tractors, all Allis WCs (see? over the years I've even learned that they are Allis WCs!), and have continued to find ever more reasons to do so. For example, in my little town of 320 people I always enjoyed the company of friends like Kenny Porath and Al Schmitt, mechanics; Don Hochstetler, machinist; Dennis Adams, auto body repairman; Dan Selden, plumber and handyman; Mel Halsey and Bud Stoeger, amateur but thoroughly experienced tractor repairmen. But now when I encounter these old friends, we don't have to talk about the weather. We have new common ground—valve seats, shifter forks, water pump seals, and steering sectors. My old pals have become even better friends than they were before—which is why this book is dedicated to them—because they have been so completely generous with information it took them years of busted knuckles to learn. Instead of laughing at my ignorance and wish to learn in the late years of my life the information they have acquired since their youth, they appreciate that I am interested in learning and that I value their wisdom.

I have made a world of new friends, people who have sent me old tractor

Derelict Fantasy

From The Nebraska Farmer, *"The Liar's Corner," 1992*

Fifteen years ago a friend gave me a derelict 1937 Allis Chalmers WC tractor. Okay, it's not much of a tractor in comparison with the monsters that prowl the fields today but I like Sweet Allis because it's almost exactly my age, because it starts every time I grab the crank and twist, and—get this—because it started the very first time I saw it, a year or so after it had been left sitting in a weed patch behind a friend's farm.

Okay, so I love this old tractor. In fact, I love it so much, I bought brand-new tires for it last fall, so the rubber is worth more than the machine. And a couple weeks ago I bought another 1937 Allis WC for parts, just in case, even though Sweet Allis, as she has come to be called, has given us no evidence of needing transplants.

So now I have two tractors to find parts for. But here's the question: in my experience, I've never found a 1937 Allis WC that doesn't run! I have this recurring dream that eventually I will be out looking for a parts Allis to cannibalize for my other two, and at an auction maybe, I buy a piece of junk that has been pushed into a ravine. Nothing is left but the frame, about half the engine block submerged under water with two of the spark plugs out, nothing of the transmission, and two of the four wheels. Someone has shot the radiator full of holes and the wiring—mostly baling wire to begin with—is snarled up like a ball of twine.

In my fantasy, I buy the mess for $25, hook on a chain and drag it out of the muck. On the way up the slope, the crank accidentally catches on a tree stump, turns half a turn, and the darned thing starts up and drives itself up the rest of the way and right onto the equipment trailer.

manuals, given me advice, sold me parts, shared experiences, and—get this—given me tractors. Several old timers have sensed my affection for the Allis WC and have simply said, "I have one I too have loved; rather than letting her rust away, you come and get her and show her some of the love and care she deserves in her old age."

One of the most remarkable of my gift tractors was one I got for giving a speech at Swedish Days in Stromsburg, Nebraska. Shari Sundberg of Stromsburg wrote me a couple years ago asking if I would give a presentation—one of the ways I scratch out a living is giving banquet and program speeches. I showed the letter to my wife Lovely Linda and said, "I can tell from the note that while these are nice folks, they don't have any money for this program and it's probably outside, which I hate." So, I wrote to Shari and told her I wouldn't be able to be a part of their festivities.

She wrote back that I was indeed right—they didn't have any money, and the program was outdoors, and she understood quite well my unwillingness to take on the job. She was especially sorry, she said, however, because her husband Roger had planned on giving me his 1934 Allis Chalmers WC at the program, thinking maybe I could drive my new machine in the parade that day.

EEEEEK! Put 'er in reverse! "Well, Ms. Sundberg, as it turns out, I looked over my calendar and it isn't as clogged as I thought, and maybe it won't be as hot as it sometimes is in June, and maybe the wind won't blow, and maybe I won't swallow fifty bugs." (As I stood on the stage the evening of the program, a bird did poop with remarkable and admirable accuracy directly into the cup of Seven-Up I was holding in my hand, it was stinking hot, and bugs swarmed up my nose.)

The Sundbergs were not only good to their word and delivered a nice, operating 1934 Allis Chalmers WC to our farm a couple weeks later, but they also brought with the tractor one of the most remarkable things I have ever gotten with a tractor, a video tape transferred from a late 1940s home movie film of that very tractor being used to remove snow from the great blizzard of '49! I don't very often sit and watch a video tape with my mouth agape, but on this occasion I couldn't even blink I was so thoroughly blitzed. It's like having a video of your grandmother when she was a child! You think I don't treat that tractor with love and affection?! I saw her in action when she was a pretty little school girl after all!

So, now, years after I first drained the oil from the Fantasizer, I am still hauling derelict Allis WCs into the yard. I tell Linda, "This place is not a junk yard or tractor park; this is a rest home for tired, old machines that fed our fathers and mothers!" What's goofy is that I actually believe that. (I tried telling her once that this is a tractor stud farm, where machines come to relax, but she said she'd already figured that out from the way they keep multiplying and I

The Bible According to Allis Chalmers

From The Nebraska Farmer, *"The Liar's Corner," July 1994*

A few months ago I got a letter from my Cousin Jim, blaming me for getting him and his friend, the local preacher, into trouble because I talked them into buying and working on an old tractor. Seems they bought a derelict Case VAC tractor, hauled it down main street (allegedly at the instigation of the pastor), did a thoroughly incompetent job of pulling the wool over Wife Dorothy's eyes, and THEN had the gall to try to challenge me into a pulling contest with one of my beloved and gentle Allis WCs. I presumed that once they had been thoroughly humiliated here in The Liars Corner, Jim and his perky preacher would slink away into the Sandhills.

But, nope. Here they come, back for more. Jim whines that now Dorothy won't let him put up a sign in the front yard reading, "The Glenns' Old Iron Pile." In fact, Jim writes, "She is threatening to have the city council rezone our lot. She wants to make sure that nothing that looks like a tractor will be allowed in the yard."

Jim, Jim, Jim, Jim, Jim... You've got to stop muddling along like this and take advice from old trusty Relative Rog: Tell Dorothy (and the City Council) that they are not really tractors, which in the case, so to speak, of a Case is fairly close to the truth. Tell 'em that what may look like a tractor to them is really a planter. Arrange a couple petunias tastefully around the engine and gracefully in the wheel spokes and there you are. Everyone will be happy, take my word for it

But that's not all that was in the packet from ol' Jim. Glenn Loy, Jim's preacher buddy and—get this!—spiritual guide also wrote me. First he tried to get himself in good with me: "Jim seems proud to share that he is related to you, which in itself is something. Lots of folks don't want to claim relatives. I spent a lot of time one-way-ing with a 1939 Allis WC, pulling a six-foot one-way [plow] up by Hamill, South Dakota, when I was young. Never was able to kill that engine. It would just crank up and bury itself when the plow got stuck with a rock."

Now, up to that point, the good reverend is sticking pretty close to his text. There are continued on next page folks around here who have dug house foundations and even pit silos, simply by running a chain from a WC's draw bar to a 90- or 100-ton weight, putting her in gear, popping the clutch, and letting her grind away for a day or so. But then the preacher starts to try to talk me again into torturing my WCs. (I hope he has better arguments for tithing for next Sunday's sermon!) "My WC threatened to run over me if I ever passed up any chance to let it show up a John Deere or International in a tractor pull. Now, you probably don't know this, but letting a WC enter a pulling contest is Scriptural. Hezekiah 6:8 says, 'Thou shalt never waste the energy and enthusiasm of an Allis WC by passing up a pulling contest.'"

I'm more of a literary than biblical scholar, of course, so my references run more to Andrew Marvell's 1657 quotation, "Orange bright, Like golden lamps in a green light" (no offense meant to the Olivers and Deeres, of course), or Sir Walter Scott's "The orange flower perfumes the bower...," or even Goethe's "Knowest thou the land...where the gold orange glows in the deep thicket's gloom?"

Though I looked through my Bible pretty close, I never could find that Hezekiah text. I did, however, find what might be a relevant citation in Restorations WD-40: "Yea, though thou be anointest with the oil of the Rumely and the curse of the metric wrench be on thee, yea, though ye walk through the valley of the shadow of debt, let your pastures bloom with the golden flowers of Allis. Peace will be in your household again if ye but let your steel minions take their rest. Labor in the cool of your shade trees, ye mechanics of Old Iron; shun the noise and furor of the arena, ye Sons of Snap-On. And lo! the sweet daughters of Nebraska, Linda and Dorothy alike, will silence their complaining and serve ye cold beer and ham sandwiches even unto the heat of the day."

Okay, now that I've set Jim and Glenn straight about the Bible and tractor pulling, I guess we can move along, huh? But not very far. In another column I commented on a newspaper clipping Wilbur Rahan sent me about a mysterious orphan Allis Chalmers tractor that showed up in an Antelope County pasture. Sheriff Ralph Black was looking for the owner. Well, a concerned Antelope County citizen, Bill Beed, wrote me, pretty upset about the whole situation. He writes, "Sheriff Ralph still has this Allis in his custody. In fact, the last time I saw the tractor, it was in an impound yard, just like a common criminal—no shed, not even a shade tree. I'll bet he even towed it in with a John Deere or a Case or maybe even his Bronco. I'm sure I'll be in trouble with Sheriff Ralph for exposing this injustice, but I thought the public should know."

Well, I figured I would turn the power of the press on this issue and put in an immediate call to Sheriff Ralph Black in Neligh. The lady who answered the phone was very courteous but pleaded innocence. She said they did indeed have the tractor but she knew nothing about it. I called again the next day. Sheriff Black was still out rounding up Antelope County miscreants, but the lady said that he had made special effort just that morning to throw a warm blanket over the orange old-timer sitting out there in the impound yard. On my third call, I reached Deputy Darrell Hamilton, who gave me a full report. He said that they had finally found the owner of the tractor and he had received a stern lecture about the responsibilities of tractor ownership. As it turns out, the WD was neither stolen or abandoned, it was only a runaway. Apparently, a breeze had pushed the starter button enough to turn the engine over and start it up. The tractor had then wandered around the countryside (it being the mating season and all), finally winding up in the middle of the Antelope County field with a bad cough and hopelessly lost.

dropped the argument as counterproductive.)

I suspect that every collector and restorer of old tractors—any kind of old tractors—tells pretty much the same stories of adventure, trial, woe, and joy. Frankly, I think God takes care not only of babies and drunks but also folks who restore old tractors. A couple months ago I was speaking to a group in Corpus Christi, Texas, and who should show up but Gene Ball, an old friend of mine from Meteetse, Wyoming. And he had a paper grocery sack in his arms. We gave him a bad time about his still using the same old luggage and then he said, "I was at a garage sale in Meteetse earlier this summer, saw this stuff, and just knew it would be useful to you, Rog."

It was twenty pounds of operating manuals, parts books, guides, and papers dealing with old tractors, most of them Allis Chalmers—a treasure trove. As I looked through the pages, I found exactly the materials I needed to work on a magneto I had been plugging away at (you should excuse the pun) trial-and-error for months—but that's another story I'll tell you later. Thing is, what seemed to be strictly by accident, I suddenly wound up with precisely the sheets of information I needed.

And my next stop on that particular trip was Milwaukee, where I stepped outside the fancy hotel I was staying in, and surveyed the four taxi cabs sitting at the curb. One was driven by a guy with a turban, the second sported a sombrero hanging from the rearview mirror, and the third had sounds of rap music booming through the closed windows. In the fourth cab a fat, unshaven old guy slept soundly with his mouth open; I rapped on his window. "Are you free?" I asked.

"See anyone in here with me?" he grumped.

"Ever work at the Allis plant in West Allis?" I asked.

"Naw, I never could get on, but my Old Man worked there forty years."

"How would you feel about taking me out there and showing me around the old factory grounds an hour or two?"

"Get in here, boy," he grinned, and we spent a morning, him showing me everything I ever wanted to know about the hallowed ground where the tractors I love so much rolled off the assembly line. You don't get that sort of joy from collecting salt shakers or baseball cards, I bet.

And it's all these personal, idiosyncratic experiences that have made me not only a dabbler in tractor rebuilding but a man totally in love with my Allis WCs. What's so good about Allis WCs? Actually, nothing. Minneapolis-Molines, John Deeres, Fords, Cockshutts, Cases, Hubers...it makes no difference. I'd try to give you advice on how to choose a make of tractor to restore but chances are, a make of tractor will choose you. It will be the kind of tractor your grandfather drove, or maybe the very tractor your grandfather drove if you're especially lucky. Maybe it'll be a gift, like Sweet Allis, or a chance bargain at an auction sale, or a tractor whose color your wife likes (it's always a good idea to do whatever you can to make this all seem like something you're doing for your wife). And perhaps I should add at this point that this volume will certainly seem to some like a hopeless throw-back to the politically incorrect days of unregenerate male chauvinism, but the fact of the matter is, 99 out of 100 tractor restorers in my experience are men. God bless those of you who are ladies; there's surely a special place in heaven for you.

If you're not already far enough into this process to realize it, tractor restoration is a passion in the very real sense of that word. I was once at a tractor show watching a proud gent carefully roll his fully and beautifully restored Allis WC off the truck bed to take it to the exhibit area. He took a handkerchief from his pocket and gently flicked some road dust from the manifold. I turned to his wife and said, "I'll bet he doesn't treat you like that."

Somewhat wistfully she replied, "He used to."

Chapter One

Getting Started ◆

One day, shortly after acquiring The Fantasizer and facing some mainte-nance work on Sweet Allis, I was up in the town tavern talking with my auto body repairman buddy Dennis "Bondo" Adams. "Well," I said, "I think I'll go down and get started working on the tractor."

"Oh, Rog," he gasped in mock horror (or maybe even real horror). "You're not going to...to...to tinker, are you?!"

And for a year that's about what I did...tinker. But somewhere along the line I mentioned in my humor column in the *Nebraska Farmer* magazine that I had a couple Allis WCs and was enjoying tinkering on them. A kind old gent not far from here wrote to me that he had an old Allis WC and if I was interested, he might be willing to sell it. I probably wouldn't have been very excited about the idea— the old-iron bug

still hadn't bitten me hard—but for two things he wrote in his letter: he said 1) he had bought the tractor new in 1935, so I would be the second owner, and 2) it had been sitting untouched in a shed for over twenty years.

I asked Bondo if he could bring his big trailer and go with me to take a look at this machine, and he said he would. We found the farmer and went out in his yard to open that dusty old shed. We almost had to dismantle the door because it hadn't been opened in decades. "Look her over and see if it's something you'd be interested in," the old-timer offered.

Of course, there was nothing I could do from that moment on; one of my daughters is adopted and I still laugh when I remember the day we went to pick her up as a baby at the orphanage. "Would you like to take a look at this baby and decide if she's what you want?" the social worker asked. Jeez, how can you look at a baby and say no?! Well, same way with an old tractor.

There she sat, covered in decades of dust, but in pretty good condition, considering. We aired up the tires and they held just fine. We pulled her out of the shed into the sunlight for the first time since Bondo was a little boy and looked her over. Everything was there—carb, mag, fenders, radiator. No obvious holes, no broken castings, no split in the block. We turned at the crank. Hmmm. Pretty solid. "Yeah," the farmer said. "The motor may be stuck. In fact, I think that's why I pulled her into the shed."

I suppose I had some uneasiness about that. What does one do about a stuck motor? Is a stuck motor a shot motor? Is a stuck motor anything like a frozen engine? Well, there are lots of things to be said about that, things I would eventually learn:

1) tractor engines "stick," auto engines "freeze";

2) in fact, tractors don't have "engines," they have "motors";

3) it's the rare tractor motor that hasn't been turned over in twenty years that isn't stuck;

4) it's a lot more fun working on a stuck motor than one that runs just fine;

5) the cheeriest words you will hear from a prospective seller or auctioneer is, "The motor is stuck." (As buyer, you turn your head slightly to one side, suck in a lot of air, close one eye, and look at that motor with suspicion. "Stuck motor, huh?" you say. "Tsk tsk tsk. Don't like the sound of that. Could be a real problem. Stuck motor. Well. I guess she might still be worth something for parts or scrap iron.")

Folks, a stuck motor is about as bad a flaw as that cute little mole on Cindy Crawford's left cheek. But we'll get to that later (stuck motors, not Cindy Crawford).

But I didn't know all that at that time—I knew about Cindy Crawford and her mole but not about stuck tractor motors, I mean. What pushed me over the edge was when the old farmer went to the house and brought out his original operator's manual, the one that came with the tractor when he bought it, still in perfect condition. "Goes with the tractor," he said. What the heck. There are a lot worse ways to spend $250. "Sold," I said.

Was $250 a fair price for that tractor? What is a fair price? About the only constant in old tractor prices is the price of scrap iron. At the moment, it's three or four cents a pound. An Allis WC weighs 3,000 pounds, so at the very bottom, the thing is worth $90–100 at a junkyard. The most likely pieces to break down and therefore the most likely to be scavenged from a derelict tractor are the magneto and carburetor or, on newer models, the starter and generator. The most likely parts to be broken on an old tractor are the gas filter, gauges, and radiator. The most likely to be rusted out are wheels (decayed from sinking into the ground or from leaking saline solution often left in the tires), toolbox, battery box, fuel tanks (there may be more than one), and air cleaner. The most likely body parts to be missing from a tractor as a result of normal farm usage are the grill and fenders.

You've got to figure that if you go to a junkyard or parts store, you're going to pay a handsome price for most of those items, precisely because they are the most in demand—$25–50 for a carb or mag, $50 for a pair of fenders, and you may never find a replacement for a missing or broken temperature gauge, no matter what the price. So if they are present and in passable condition on the tractor you're looking over, you sure want to consider that in what you are willing to pay. This old girl I was looking at, later to be named "The Giltner" after the town where we got it, had all those things and they all appeared to be in pretty good condition, except the gauges. Heck, I could take off the fenders, carb, mag, and wheels, sell the rest for scrap iron (perish the thought) and still come out ahead.

Roger's Rules for Collecting Old Iron
(and Living with Your Spouse)

From Successful Farming, *February 1993*

There's more to collecting and restoring old tractors than nuts and bolts. A *lot* more. In fact, nuts and bolts are the least of it. Ask our marriage counselor. Don't get me wrong: Lovely Linda is a wonderful wife and friend and she has endured more than any one woman should have to put up with. I'm the first to admit that life with me isn't easy. I admit that, though I don't always believe it.

Things got tense when I began collecting Allis Chalmers WC tractors. I had one WC for almost twenty years before it occurred to me that it might be nice to have two. And once I had two, I thought it would really be handy to have a couple of junk WCs around for parts, but along with the parts tractors I got a couple of "runners." So then there were six. And I got a good deal on one that had been sitting in a shed for nearly twenty-five years, and I think I have another couple lined up not far from here, if I can just work out the details. It has taken the better part of two years but just last week Lovely Linda finally sighed, "I give up. I've lost track. I have no idea how many tractors you have." It was a moment of triumph—but it was not without, as they say, its downside.

Over the past couple years, I have collected advice along with my WCs, and I think it is only neighborly that I pass along to you what I have learned. If you're married and are thinking about getting into the old iron business, forget trivial things like socket wrenches and bearing pullers and lay the groundwork for your new hobby by carefully studying the following rules...THE WELSCH RULES OF TRACTOR COLLECTING!

RULE #1. Collect only one model and make of tractor—nothing but John Deere Bs or Allis Chalmers Gs, for example. When all your tractors are the same color and shape, it's harder, if not impossible, for anyone (if you catch my drift) to figure out how many tractors you actually have.

RULE #2. Similarly, never line up your tractors, ever. Nothing distresses a difficult spouse more than seeing twelve old tractors lined up, looking for all the world like a burning pile of hundred dollar bills. Scatter the tractors around—a couple behind the shed, one or two in the shed, another beside the garage—so that it is not possible for anyone, if you know who I mean, to see more than two or three from any one perspective. Your hobby will be less "irritating" that way, if you know what I mean.

RULE #3. For much the same reason, don't number your tractors #1, #2, #3. Give them names. You'd be surprised how much less trouble you will have, if you talk about "Steel Wheels" or "Sweet Allis" rather than "Allis Chalmers WC #14."

RULE #4. Somewhere fairly early in your collecting, buy a tractor you don't want. Sell it again as quickly as you can; don't worry about making money on the transaction. The main thing is to get a tractor and get rid of it. Then, for years, you can say, "Yes, Angel-face, I do have six John Deere Bs, and they are in the shed while our car is out in the weather, but that doesn't mean that I will *always* have six John Deere Bs. *Remember the one I got rid of a few years ago? I'm thinking of selling another one any day now so we can put the car in the garage.*"

If you are lucky enough to have a friend who collects tractors, make an arrangement for him to drop off a tractor now and again. That way you can say—if anyone asks—that you bought it. Then have it hauled off again, and say you sold it. With this system, you can re-establish your reputation for moderation every couple of years or so.

WARNING: About the time I accumulated my sixth or seventh Allis WC I thought I'd be smart, so I bought a lovely little Allis C. Linda and our nine-year-old daughter Antonia were standing in the farm yard as I unloaded this lovely little item that needed only some wheel work and a new wiring harness. "I see you bought yourself another tractor that doesn't run," said Linda.

"Guess what, dear?" I beamed. "I didn't buy myself another Allis Chalmers. I bought *you* an Allis Chalmers! She's yours, and ain't she cute?"

I could tell by the look on her face that she was about as excited as she was the Christmas I gave her a new drain cleaner attachment for her vacuum sweeper, but I wasn't at all prepared for what she said next: "How much can I get for it?"

"Er, uh, I didn't get it for you to sell, honey-cakes. I was thinking…if you don't want to drive it all the time, I can take it into town now and then just to keep the oil stirred up for you. It won't be any trouble at all."

"Well, thanks, Rog, you're really too sweet. I don't deserve a darling like you. How much can I get for it?"

I almost broke into tears at the thought of someone loading that great tractor onto a trailer and driving off with it. I was thinking that I should have gone with my first impulse and said that it had followed me home and could I maybe keep it, but thank goodness, about that time my mind kicked into road gear. "Actually, I thought that if you wouldn't mind sharing, it could also be Antonia's tractor. Right. That's it! Eventually it'll be Antonia's tractor."

Antonia leaped into the C's seat with a squeal and started twisting the steering wheel and making tractor noises. Linda snorted something about me fixing my own supper that night—that is, if I was intending to stay over—and headed back toward the house while I helped Antonia bond with her tractor. That was a close call, and my advice to you is not to buy your wife a tractor. Better stick with a drain cleaner attachment for the vacuum sweeper.

RULE #5. Pay for tractors with a cashier's check, postal money order, or cash, which leave far less evidence than checks drawn on the family account. Once you have gotten possession of a tractor and paid for it, *eat the stubs, carbon copies, or receipts immediately.* Such things have a way of becoming an embarrassment later, take it from me.

Some collectors like to point out to skeptical marriage partners that what with interest rates so low these days, buying old tractors is actually an investment, a way of being sure the spouse will be "taken care of and comfortable should something…something terrible happen." Doesn't work with Lovely Linda. She thinks Allis Chalmers WCs are the "something terrible."

RULE #6. Now and then buy a wreck "for parts," even if you don't need the parts, even if there are no salvageable parts. In fact, you might want to consider hauling home a wreck or two whenever you haul home a good machine—if possible, on the same trailer or truck. This is called "liability averaging." If your spouse says something about it being strange that you have money for yet another tractor but not enough for a new refrigerator, point indignantly to the tractors on the trailer—the beautiful one on steel and in running condition for which you paid $1,600 and the two rusted hulks you got for $50 each—and you huff (or whine, depending on what has worked in the past), "Snookums, I got those for a little

continued on next page

more than $500 each and the one in the back is easily worth $2,000 just as it stands, a tidy profit of $400, more than four times what I paid for the other two." See? Doesn't that make you sound like an investment wizard?

Some collectors find it effective to add something like, "It's pretty hard to find a good refrigerator for $500!" but it has been my experience that a smart-aleck attitude can fairly directly lead to the purchase of a $500 refrigerator.

RULE #7. When things get critical in the household, you might consider dragging home a tractor without a transmission or rear wheels. If there is a complaint, you say something like, "Tractor? What tractor? That's not a tractor! That's only a front end. Not even close to a tractor."

Then a couple weeks later bring home a rear end, minus the radiator, engine, and front wheels. "What tractor?" you say. "That's no tractor! That's only a rear end. Not even close to a tractor." Don't try this, however, more than once every couple years.

RULE #8. Have an implement dealer or friend call you now and then when you're not at home and tell your spouse, "Rog told me to keep an eye on the Allis WC going at the auction up at Centerville Saturday, but it sold for $1,200 and I know there's no way a financially cautious and responsible guy like Rog would pay that much so I didn't even make a bid on it for him."

Not only will this make you look real good, the next time you do buy a tractor, say something like, "Lovie-bear, this beauty only cost me $300, which means we're $900 ahead of where we'd have been if I'd gotten the one at Centerville. If I keep saving money like this, we'll be able to go on a Caribbean cruise next winter." If you say it fast enough, it might work.

RULE #9. If your mate insults your tractor work by referring to it as "rustoration" or "tinkering," laugh a light-hearted laugh that makes it clear that tractors are not to you what shoes are to Imelda Marcos.

RULE #10. In the event that your situation deteriorates to the point where your mate asks, "Who do you love more, me or your blasted tractors?" whatever you do, don't ask for time to think it over.

Notes

The above suggestions are not dishonest or deceptive, exactly. They are ways to make life easier for your spouse. In fact, now that I think about it, these little acts of diplomacy are actually a kindness, a way to smooth the road for someone you love. Following Roger's Rules is a way of being a better person. People who follow Roger's Rules are *good* people. In fact, I feel so good about myself, I think I'll go out and buy myself another tractor! It'll be a good investment. I'll have it hauled in at night. That way I won't bother Linda.

But all that is a matter of logic, and if you are going to start fooling around with logic, you might just as well forget rebuilding tractors as a hobby. Jeez, if you had any brains, would you be spending any money at all on such nonsense, and endangering your life along the way? (As Lovely Linda once said, "Rog, can't you find a hobby that doesn't weigh quite so much?") I love these old Allis WCs, especially abused orphans, and here was one that needed a daddy. And here was its original owner, like a father of the bride, about to answer the question "And who gives this bride?" with the traditional answer, "Her mother and I."

And I was an eager and ardent groom. No bickering on this deal. To hell with common sense. "I'll take her, Pops," I said to the farmer.

I told you, choosing what sort of tractor to work on is a moot question in most cases because the tractor chooses you. If I had a choice, if I were starting from scratch, I think I might head in another direction. There is a story—it may be apocryphal but we're talking gossip here, not gospel, right?—that Enzo Ferrari, who originally built the great race cars, was having trouble finding a transmission that would handle the immense power of his engines. So he asked around, until finally another Italian showed up at the Ferrari shops and said that he was a tractor builder and he believed his transmissions could handle the strain.

Ferrari recoiled in indignation and snorted that he wasn't about to put a tractor transmission in his elegant motor cars and that if this guy wanted his tractor parts in a race car, he could build his own damned machine. And so he did. His name was Lamborghini and he did just fine.

When I heard that story, true or not, and knowing that I will never own a Ferrari or a Lamborghini automobile, I instantly thought about how great it would be to own...a Lamborghini tractor. As it turns out, they are not at all rare on the European market. I have a copy of the *Farmers Guide* from England in front of me at this very moment and I find for sale in the advertisements a half-dozen Lamborghinis, all fairly recent and expensive models, but if there are new ones, I'll bet there are old, battered ones too, just aching to be pulled into a shop and put back in action.

See? If I had thought about it, I'd probably have gotten an old Lamborghini tractor or two. Or maybe a Porsche. In Lincoln, Nebraska, at this very moment, there is an antique, one-cylinder Porsche tractor for sale for $2,500. And there is the very good likelihood that machine will never be worth less than what you pay for it today. How much is that new car you bought last year worth today?

I'd love to be able to tell people, "Yeah, my day-to-day vehicle is a Porsche. An open-wheeled job. I love to open it up in high gear and go up the highway into town at top speed just to hear the engine hum and watch people's heads turn." But...the Porsche in Lincoln has a problem that is to me the worst possible thing one can find wrong with an antique tractor: it has been restored to perfect condition. Someone has used up all the fun of the tractor by rebuilding it himself. He should be giving it away!

All the fun has been taken out of it for me. My fun is taking an utter derelict and making it run. Once it runs, I'm not even sure what to do with it. I recall being stunned once when I was raving on and on about how much I love restoring tractors and someone asked me, "What do you do with them when they're all fixed up?" I was flabbergasted because I'd never really thought about it. "Sell them?" Good grief, no! That's like selling your children! "Use them as farm machinery?" Are you kidding? These things are retired! To this day I don't know what to do with them, to tell you the truth. My joy is in the process, not the thing.

But there are folks who buy fully restored tractors and pretty much use them as toys. That's fine. It's just not my pleasure. My father-in-law bought a John Deere B when he was just a kid out of high school. He worked with it all his life and when he retired he decided to treat himself and his B to a full restoration. He took it to a garage and had the job done to a fare-thee-well. It sits in his garage now while his late model car sits in the driveway. I can understand that. He loves that tractor but rebuilding it just wasn't something he would enjoy. He loves the tractor, not the process of redoing it. So now he enjoys it. And you have to grant him that pleasure. After all, this poor guy has a son-in-law...well, never mind.

These days I'm pickier about what I pay for Allis WCs. I have enough tractors to work on for a long time and enough "parts tractors" to keep me supplied for the rest of my life, so now I pick up another machine only when the price is right (the last three I acquired were gifts), when the tractor is in particularly good shape (not running but with clean sheet metal and good carb or mag), or if it has something particularly interesting about it (more about that later). You've got to keep in mind what money is doing these days: the Country Store Christmas catalog carries a 1/16 scale model of a 1939 Allis-Chalmers WC tractor on steel wheels for—gasp, choke—$179.98. This toy tractor costs substantially more than you'd have to pay for the real thing! Go figure.

I do think it might be worth your time to consider, before you get into this too far, 1) what you want to do, 2) why you are doing it, and 3) for whom you are doing it. If you are going to restore your grandfather's tractor and park it in your suburban garage as a symbolic tribute to that fine old man, then you may not want to build much of a shop; one tractor scarcely seems worth the trouble and expense, right? If you are going to work on more than one tractor down the line, are you going to work on whatever tractors come along? Or two-cylinder tractors of various makes? Only John Deeres—but any model of the Greenies you can find? Only John Deere Bs? Crawlers? Diesels? You can make your work later on a lot easier if you think about what your direction might be now. Since I work only on Allis Chalmers WCs, I don't need the shop manual for the model G I run across at an auction sale, but I might as well buy that WC magneto because I will probably need it for the next WC I pull into the shop even though I may not need it now. Or, I may buy the manual because a friend needs the manual and has a set of WC transmission bearings I need and can trade him for.

Me, I have decided to work on one model of tractor, the Allis Chalmers WC. I can imagine that some folks might be bored by working on the same model tractor over and over and over, but since I started with such enormous mechanical ignorance, I feel that in the twenty years or so I have for such work, it will be all I can do to master...if ever I get that far...this one model. Besides, it sure makes buying and locating parts a lot easier. And believe me, I have never been bored, working on that one model; every Allis WC I have worked on offers a completely new personality and unique set of problems and treasures.

When I started, I decided to work only on "unstyled" WCs, the ones with square radiators and plain, barrel gas tanks. But then somewhere along the line I bought or accepted a WC sight unseen and it turned out to be styled— rounded hood, bullet gas tank, slim profile fenders (although everything else is still pretty much the same aside from that sheet metal). And I decided, okay, I'll take on styled WCs, too. And then I bought a model C Allis for Antonia. And now I know I'd like a WD or WD-45, and I sure wouldn't pass up a G if I found one cheap. So, my early plans haven't locked me into anything; they just gave me some direction in building my shop, buying tools, picking up parts, accumulating a library, that sort of thing.

Healthy Choices
From Successful Farming

I have been in this business of restoring old tractors for, oh, almost a whole year now, so I pretty much know everything there is to know. And I am fully prepared to share all that information. No sense in us both making the same mistakes.

The most important, most frequent question about tractor restoration is, "Why?" (Or, in the case of my wife Lovely Linda, "WHY?!!!") My own reasons range from cosmetic (I find that after a day lying under a tractor, putting on an oil pan maybe, my hair takes on new body and luster) to philosophical (uh...).

Why tractors? Because you can work on them standing up, for one thing, and for a guy of my age and build, that's really important. Why *old* tractors? Because there's none of that foreign metric nonsense with old tractors, just good ol' American inches, pounds, hairs, and smidgins.

In fact, with old tractors there are not even problems with all that electrical stuff like amps and volts that nobody understands anyway. (Ask a scientist what electricity is. The answer will be something like, "Uh, it's like water, sort of but not really, and it flows through wire, even though there's no hole in the wire, and it makes things turn, but we aren't sure how, and, hey, lick your fingers and hold onto this spark plug wire.")

On an Allis WC there are exactly four wires, one leading to each spark plug. Even that can be confusing occasionally for a guy like me, but four wires is within the grasp, I think, of my eventual electrical skills. With old tractors, you didn't hook up a computer to figure out what was going on inside: one of my ancient Allis Chalmers manuals shows how to brace up a tree limb so you can pull the engine on your nineteen-horsepower beast. It was understood by the manufacturer that these machines were going to be worked on out under a cottonwood tree by a guy who owned three wrenches, a claw hammer, and a bent screwdriver—which is to say, me.

Of course, while you don't *need* a lot of tools, a big part of restoring old tractors is buying tools. There's not a man alive, and only a few women, who wouldn't be perfectly happy buying a NAPA store or Snap-On truck, closing its doors to the public, and spending a lifetime admiring and inventorying all those neat, shiny tools. Having a "shop" for restoring tractors is a lot like owning a NAPA or Snap-On franchise. Except without all the trouble of customers.

In fact, tractor restoration is a great economic alternative for these times when your $500,000 in certificates of deposit or gold bullion just isn't paying off the way you think it should. Say you buy a junked John Deere B for $500, haul it into your $5,000 shop, and use your $2,000 worth of tools to take it apart and start repairs. You put about $2,500 worth of parts into it and a few hundred dollars of liquids and gooey things. You invest a couple thousand hours of labor and a few thousand dollars for medical treatment (burns, busted knuckles, stomach pumping for the time you poured the Mountain Dew on a stuck tappet and drank the Liquid Wrench), and before you know it, you have transformed a $500 piece of green junk into a $1,200 showpiece, thus more than doubling your initial investment. Where else can you get that kind of return on your buck? Isn't America great?!

A remarkable proportion of time spent on restoration consists of sitting or standing around and staring. Take auction sales, for example. That's where you get old tractors. Well, not exactly. It's not where *you* get old tractors, it's where other people get old tractors. See, you can go to all the sales you want, but you will never buy a tractor. They always go too high. Always. If you take $300 to Fleischblum's sale, the tractor there will go for $310. If you take $350 to Kosmolinski's sale, their tractor will go for $360. On the other hand, the next time you talk with your buddy Lunchbox, he'll say, "Kosmolinski's? You shoulda been at the sale over at Grembeck's. His WC, never spent a night out of the shed, went for $35, with a spare set of wheels."

Thing to do is to tell Lunchbox that the next time he sees a WC going for less than $300, he should pick it up for you. He will, but funny thing, it will always cost you exactly $300. He's bidding on a tractor for you at Freeble's auction where WCs are going for $300 while you stand in Widow Dinkster's farmyard and stare as her WC goes for $8,222. I don't know why. That's just the way it works.

When you're not standing and staring at auction sales, you'll be standing and staring at parts stores ("Now, was that a 9/32ths-inch bolt three and 3/8ths inches long, or a 3/8ths-inch bolt 32 inches long?"); at tractor manuals ("Insufficient clearance shims in the crush shell will result in spontaneous destruction of the engine within the first minute of operation, so torque all castellated nuts to 22.2 square foot-pounds on quarter inch lugs, 47.3 inch-ounces on 37/64 inch lugs, or else"); and at your wife ("What do you mean, 'What will I do with it if I ever get it running?'").

I think it's the standing and staring part that's good for blood pressure. (Yours, not your wife's.)

Finally, old tractors are good tractors because they have only forty-six parts. (Okay, some tractors have a few more, some a few less, but forty-six parts is a good working number.) The frame of an Allis WC is two nine-foot long pieces of angle iron with some holes in them. And that's it. I understand the frame on an Allis WC. I not only understand a WC's water pump, I can find a WC's water pump. Try that in your BMW. This past winter I completely dismantled an Allis WC, touching every single part in it, all forty-six of them. And I put it back together. No, it doesn't run, but at this point in my restoration career, "running" is not the most important thing in the world.

And that leads into the next question—why? If your intention is to make some money by taking a wreck and rebuilding it into a collector's prize, I imagine you'll want everything to be precisely accurate and take as little time as possible to get a return on your investment. (And as I said when my first wife dumped me, announcing that she wanted "to find herself," "Boy, are you going to be disappointed!")

If you're rebuilding Grandpa's old Fordson, you probably intend to restore it to the condition you or he best remembers. I have found with my unstyled Allis WCs with "flat" fenders, for example, that someone must have discovered pretty early on that a Ford Model A running board fits precisely between the back fenders and over the small platform over the PTO shaft. And that is precisely where you would like to have something to stand on, something to help you up into the seat, something for a passenger to stand on, something to put a lunch box or toolbox on. So, a lot of farmers did just that—bolted or welded an old Model A running board between those fenders. Now, what's most accurate—the way that tractor came from the factory or the way Grandpa—and a lot of other farmers like him—modified that baby? Depends on what you think, and maybe Grandpa.

Your timing may depend on who you're doing this for too. You may want to get your restoration job of Grandpa's tractor done in time for him to share your efforts while he can still appreciate it. Or, if he's gone, you may have all the time in the world, since the final product will mean the most to you and your family.

Your reason for doing all this work and spending all this time and money better be self-satisfaction. I haven't found much else in this hobby that counts or matters.

And that's another consideration: for whom are you going through all this work? In my case, it's for me. All my shop work is for my own pleasure in these old machines (except in those few cases where I am doing it as a response to a fun challenge, in which case it is still a matter of my own pleasure). That means I'm in no hurry and I'm not all that concerned with historical accuracy. My love is for the mechanics of the tractor, not museum work, so I have to date done absolutely nothing with bodywork and paint jobs. A few years from now I may be meticulously rubbing down Persian Orange paint to a mirror-finish and dinking out even the slightest dents in ancient fenders, but right now, that's not my thing. And I am doing this for me, so that's the way it's going to be. A few years ago it would never have occurred to me that I would be learning to weld; this year I started to learn how to weld. Not because someone told me I should, but because I want to.

Some restorers—I like to call myself a repairer or rebuilder rather than restorer—dedicate their work to competition, from outdoing another restorer, a neighbor, a friend, to winning a restorer's show at the fair or machinery show. That's okay, too. Despite my joking about tractor pullers who rebuild their old tractors for maximum power, frankly, it's none of my business. If that's what you want to do with your tractor, what business is it of mine? It's your tractor, and your work, and your pleasure.

I still think that what's important is what all this means to you; if it gives you pleasure, what you do in the privacy of your own shop with your own tractor is strictly between you and your machine. When someone comes into my shop and makes some remark to the effect that I am not being meticulously accurate, or that even though I've made the thing run, it still looks like junk, I shrug my shoulders and say something like, "Your wife's kinda ugly too, but that's your problem, now, isn't it?"

When Bondo Adams and I hauled The Giltner WC with the stuck motor into the yard, there was no question about dumping in a couple pints of gas and popping the clutch. The Giltner was stuck but good. A few friends joined us and we stood there drinking beer and staring for a while. (Though mechanicking had not yet crossed my mind, a few years ago I read a great book called *Truck* by John Jerome; one of the brightest things John J said in this book that's full of bright things is that a large part of any project like rebuilding a truck—or building a log house or working on a marriage—is standing there staring.) And the staring helps. It's true. So we stood there and stared.

We tugged at the crank and rocked the wheels. Not the slightest hint of a budge. We discussed what might loosen up the stuck piston, if it was a stuck piston and not a bearing, valve, pushrod, or whatever else was inside all that iron. I already knew that it is not a good idea to use force right off the bat—pulling the tractor behind a tractor and repeatedly popping the clutch, banging at the wheels, applying mechanical pressure to the crankshaft. Some advisors said we should pour some kerosene into the spark plug holes, some said transmission fluid, some commercial penetrating oils like Mystery Oil, WD-40, or Liquid Wrench. One guy swore by Coca Cola. On this occasion, we settled on kerosene.

I squirted about a cup's worth into each spark plug hole and let her sit a month or so. Still nothing. Mel Halsey came down with his compressor and we tried to move the pistons with air. Nothing. More kerosene. Some Liquid Wrench. Not the slightest hint of movement in the crankshaft. Finally, at a wild moment, I did something I had never done before, never so much as imagined doing in my previous fifty years of life: I took the head off the engine. At the time I considered it a crazy, even reckless thing to do—but after all I had nothing to lose. Someone was going to have to take that head off; we'd never get the thing loose without taking the head off. On the surface, it looked like a simple operation.

The only complication that had me concerned was the one oil line that ran from the filter up to a fitting on the head. I turned a brass fitting and…good grief, just like that, it was off. The valve cover (I had no idea what it was called at that time) came off quickly with the removal of four nuts. And there were the rocker arms and valve stems. I know nothing about engines but I have some idea how valves work, and it wouldn't take a genius to look at the rocker arms and figure out how they operate. No mysteries here either. I took off the twelve nuts that hold the head to the block and with enormous trepidation—would a bunch of parts fly out, I wondered? Jeez, I didn't know!—I stood atop the frame and pulled the head from the block.

Well, hmmm, look at that. There are the valves, obvious as can be, and there are the cylinder holes, and I suppose those filthy things down there are the pistons, and man, there's no question why they won't go up and down! This thing is full of dirt and black stuff and hard junk and all sorts of things that obviously don't belong in there—mouse poop, walnut shells, hunks of rust, little pieces of iron.

At this point I hauled the tractor into a shed where I could work out of the weather. And I bought an inexpensive set of socket wrenches, which I still use. At that point things got a lot more serious. I wanted to know more about what made these old girls run so I could fix this one, but more importantly, I was going through the same feelings I had experienced when I worked on the Fantasizer and Sweet Allis—a thorough pleasure in solving little problems and cleaning up a battered queen.

Now I did something very smart, which is not my usual style. I really didn't want to damage this tractor by doing something stupid (I think I was still pretty impressed that I was her second owner), which was almost certain, since I didn't have the slightest notion what I was doing. I couldn't see spending months—years? I didn't know—working on this thing, feeling the same fear every time I removed a part that I had felt when I pulled that head. So, I wondered, how could I learn about this tractor, the Allis Chalmers WC, without damaging this tractor, The Giltner?

I got every published shop manual I could for this machine, resources I'll discuss later in this book. Friends like Dan Selden loaned me their old textbooks from high school shop class. I asked mechanics questions, but their experience was not often with ancient machines like mine. So I went to a salvage yard and found a real wreck of an Allis WC, which I picked up for less than $100. I pulled it into the shop next to The Giltner. As I contemplated pulling the oil pan on The Giltner, for example, I first removed the oil pan from the parts tractor. I cleaned the pan and looked over what was inside. I oiled the pan, sealed it in a plastic bag, and put it on a shelf. And then I knew what to do when I pulled the pan off The Giltner and, as a bonus, had a clean, spare oil pan.

When I was about to remove the water pump from The Giltner, I first took the water pump from the parts machine, dismantled it, cleaned it, looked it over, and replaced whatever parts it needed (consulting with a shop manual and more experienced friends at every stage). If I was successful (which was almost always the case, not because I'm a mechanical genius but because these things don't require a mechanical genius and I had the advice of experts and printed resources), I put the unit on the parts shelves. If I wasn't successful, well, I really hadn't lost anything, after all, and I knew better than to make the same mistake with The Giltner.

Eventually, I dismantled the entire parts tractor, acquiring a world of information and a modest inventory of spare parts worth a lot more than $100.

Over the next couple months I cautiously, almost fearfully, took piece by piece off The Giltner. I removed all but one piston, and it was clearly the one that was the problem—rock-hard stuck. It took me almost two months to get that stuck piston out of the block, and then it came out complete with the shattered liner or "sleeve" of that cylinder. But it did come out. We had champagne that night before supper. I was on top of the world.

And I was completely hooked.

I worked on The Giltner for over a year. Knowing so little about engines, transmissions, or anything having to do with tractors, I spent a lot of time sitting in our town's social center, Eric's Big Table Tavern, consulting with the community's experts. As a result, everyone in town was party to the process of rebuilding that tractor. Everyone in town knew when I broke off a pan bolt, when I got it drilled out, how well I did rethreading the hole, how dumb I was when I cut off what seemed to be excessively long gaskets on the end of the oil pan, my joy when I finally got the pan on and it wasn't leaking, on and on.

About eight months into the process—I write for a living, so there were weeks when I couldn't get into my shop (to my extreme pain), there were weeks when I waited for parts, there were days when I struggled with some problem or another—I confided to Eric, "You know, pal, when I get this tractor running, I'm going to drive it up to town. I'm going to invite everyone who's helped me with the tractor to come to a champagne reception. I'm going to buy a couple cases of good champagne and plenty of good food. We'll set that tractor right outside the door and leave the door open, and we'll sit here and drink champagne, listening to that engine run."

Eric thought the proposition over a minute and said, "Uh, champagne has a shelf life of only about three years so I think I'll hold off a while before I order it, okay?"

Despite the cold water Eric threw on my ardor, I plugged away, an hour here, a day there, and finally—I was almost surprised at the moment I realized it—I was done. The last bolt had been turned, the last cover reinstalled, the last connection closed. It was a peculiar moment. I had been loving this beast for over a year by this time. I had handled almost every single part of its innards. I had thoroughly enjoyed the processes of cleaning, checking, reinstalling, replacing, repairing...and now, without warning, it was over. Talk about postpartum depression!

I was standing there staring, just as I had done before starting the job, when up drove Mel Halsey for some reason or another. "What's wrong?" he asked, reading the dismay on my face.

"It's done," I muttered.

"Well, not yet," Mel said. "You haven't started her yet. Turn her over."

"The engine's too tight to hand crank."

"Well, pour some gas in the tank and some water in the radiator and we'll give her a tow with the truck. Let's see how well you've done."

It was like a final exam. No, final exams are rarely that important. It was like taking the bar exam. No, you can always take the bar exam again if you flunk. It was like saying, "I do." Yeah, that's it. That final, that important, that emotional. We put in the gas and water. Mel hooked a chain to his pickup and back to the front pedestal of The Giltner. "Ready?" he yelled back from the cab of his truck.

I guess he didn't hear me yell back, "Hell, no..." because he eased forward into the chain and started pulling me and my companion down our farm lane. My heart pounding—I am not being overly dramatic here, believe me—I eased out the clutch. I could see the fan turn in the radiator housing. And then—my God!—the engine popped. Before I had a chance to fully enjoy the puff of smoke and oil that blew out the exhaust stack and into my face, it popped again. And again. And then it ran for a brief second. Another couple yards...and she was running. Not popping. Running.

We hadn't pulled The Giltner more than thirty yards, and it was running. Actually running. Mel stopped. I leaped from the seat and Mel came running back to meet me. We adjusted the carburetor frantically to keep the engine running. We stood back. I was grinning so hard, Mel said he was worried the corners of my mouth might meet back around my head and my scalp would fall off. Tears were running down my face. I know it's silly for a grown man, father and grandfather, to cry over an old tractor motor, but you simply cannot imagine, if you haven't been there, the incredible joy that comes from that moment when something you have worked on so hard for so long actually winds up doing what it was meant to do. It is right up there with watching your kid graduate from college with honors or seeing your book listed on a best-seller list.

I suppose a lot of people would have laughed. An old tractor engine never really sounds like a new passenger car, after all. It roars and pops, smokes and shudders. The exhaust smells terrible. Water was running from a poorly seated head gasket. An oil fitting was dripping. The fan was blowing coolant back from a loose hose clamp. Gasoline dripped from the bottom of the carburetor. Bondo Adams later eased my embarrassment by observing, "Don't worry, Rog. She's what they call a 'self-drainer.' In the winter you don't have to worry about draining all those liquids out of her because she takes care of it all herself."

True to my word, I bought champagne and cold cuts and sent out fancy invitations to all the thirty or forty people who had helped me along the way through the year. I parked The Giltner—now re-christened "Old Faithful," not so much for her faithfulness in starting as for her spouting steaming liquids for all the world like the geyser of the same name—outside Eric's door and we sat there listening, laughing, and drinking. (One friend opined, "Aren't we supposed to break a bottle of champagne over her bow?" whereupon another buddy replied, "Let's just drink the champagne and pee on the front tire!")

Everything was going fine until Jim Stromp, salvage yard operator extraordinaire, stood up—I thought, to give a toast. "You got Old Faithful running, and you deserve a lot of credit for that, Rog," he said. "But..." He raised his glass. "But, my friend, you will never...NEVER...get Silent Orville to run," and he sat back down.

Remember that tractor wreck I took apart for parts and information as I worked on The Giltner? Well, I bought several old tractors on that occasion from Jim. When we had just about finished bargaining, I pulled out my trump card: "Okay, Jim," I said, "I'll pay your price if you'll throw in the other wrecked Allis WC over there in the combines, the one with 'Silent Orville' painted on the gas tank."

Jim looked at me with confusion. He knew nothing about such a tractor. I led him through his huge salvage yard back into a cluttered lane and pointed out the tractor to him. It was half buried in dirt, a total derelict. "Sure, you can have it," Jim shrugged. And I took it. I tucked it back behind a shed, figuring I'd strip it for parts somewhere down the line since there was almost nothing about it that suggested it would ever run again.

I've had challenges in my life, but nothing like this one. It was like being slapped in the face with a leather glove by the most deadly swordsman in the land. I rose slowly from my place. Eric's Tavern was deadly silent. "I accept your challenge, Jim Stromp," I said. "Next year we will meet again at this time, at this very table, to celebrate the re-christening of Silent Orville."

Later that week I winched Silent Orv from back of the shed into the shop and started the process of tearing down a tractor and rebuilding it all over again. Of course the process is never the same twice because every restoration project has its own peculiar problems, and believe me, there were plenty of problems with Silent Orv. In fact, I put together a double-column, single-spaced, two-page list of those problems. Again I worked the year around on the tractor—never a full day, certainly not every day, not even every week. On one occasion there was a gap of almost two months when I couldn't get into the shop. But eventually, there I was again—done. I did nothing by way of real "restoration"—body work, fancy paint job, that kind of thing. My dream was simply to make that tractor run and drive again.

And again there was that magic moment when a friend—this time Mick Maun—said, "So how's Silent Orv coming along?" and I admitted that I had finished him a few weeks earlier, and Mick said, "Let's start him up." This time things did not go as swimmingly as they had with Old Faithful nee The Giltner. The tractor fired once, twice, several sporadic times but no sustained roar. We worked on the carburetor for hours. Encouraging pops, even a few seconds of running, but no cigar, as they say.

Dan Selden, something of a farm-boy, shade-tree mechanic, dropped by. "It's the carb, all right," he nodded, whereupon Mick and I looked at each other and cried in unison, "If Dan thinks it's the carb, well, there's no longer any question! It's got to be the magneto!!" We worked another couple hours on the mag with minor improvement, but nothing that suggested the breaking out of champagne.

"Dale Muhlbach," Dan said, finally. "He's a magneto expert. And I'll bet he's home."

So we loaded up Orv's magneto and several spares I had salvaged off parts tractors and we drove fifteen miles to Dale Muhlbach's farm. Dale rigged up his homemade magneto tester and we worked our way through the units we had brought with us. Sure enough, Orv's magneto was defective, firing only irregularly—pretty much like the engine had been running. But a couple of the others worked just fine. Encouraged, we put everything back into the pickup and headed back to my place. We set up the mag, timed it as Dale had recommended (a process—like almost everything else in tractor repair—that

This Is To Invite You To A Champagne And Beer Reception For

1936 Allis Chalmers WC "Silent Orv" (#22,697)

Purchased June 17, 1992
To Be ReCommissioned As "Roarin" Orv"

Said Reception To Honor Participants And Contributors To
"Roarin' Orv's" Rebuilding.

✤ ✤ ✤ ✤ ✤ ✤ ✤ ✤ ✤ ✤ ✤ ✤ ✤

September 3, 1994, Saturday, 5–6 p.m.
(at precisely 6 p.m. you're on your own)
At Eric's Big Table Tavern, Dannebrog, Nebraska

✤ ✤ ✤ ✤ ✤ ✤ ✤ ✤ ✤ ✤ ✤ ✤ ✤

By Invitation Only; Regrets Only.
Expressions Of Sympathy To Lovely Linda; Memorials To Dupah Tractor Rest Haven.
Bring A Spouse Or Love Interest, *But Not Both!!*

Please Note
That Both Jim Stromp And
Jerry Obermiller Did Assure
Me That Silent Orv Would
Never Run Again And On The
Occasion Of The
Recommissioning Of Old
Faithful, July 24, 1993, I
Vowed To Prove Them
Wrong.

Some Of Silent Orv's Problems A Year Ago:

Cracked and Goober-Welded Block • Stuck Transmission • Stuck Engine
Stuck Final Drive • Completely Shot Front End • Shot Steering Linkage
Shot Manifold • Stuck PTO • Missing Carburetor • Crushed Oil Pan
Stuck Rings • Fouled Oil Lines • Seven Sheared Pan Bolts • Fouled Valves
Stuck Tappets • Stuck Rockers • No Front Wheels • Stripped Shifter
Ruined Front Bearings and Seals • Gummed Clutch • Ruined Front Axles • Shelled Front
Bearings • Missing Fuel System Parts • Stuck Governor
Leaky Gas Tank • Dinged Hood • Shot Throttle Linkage • Stuck Rocker Arms
Shot Rear PTO Bearings • Gummed Final Drives
Cracked, Broken Steering Wheel • Ridged Sleeves • Dried, Cracked, and Leaking Seals and
Gaskets • Sheared Front End Mounting Bolts • No Plug Wires
Sheared Manifold Mount Studs • Fouled Distributor
Missing Valve Retainer Clips • Worn-Out Steering Bearings
Broken Fuel Sediment Bulb And Mount. Broke Oil Filter Mount
Out Of Order Magneto • Missing Caps And Plugs • Mis-Mounted Flywheel

seems a lot more complicated in theory and contemplation than it is in reality and application) and...there it was. Orv was roaring, whereby came his new moniker: Roarin' Orv.

Again, I was a little late with my promised party—Orv had taken fourteen months instead of the challenged twelve—but no one complained. Linda dyed a pair of white painters overalls Persian Orange for me and I drove Orv into town, flanked by daughter Antonia on her Allis C, and an honor guard of Dan Selden and Mick Maun driving Sweet Allis and Old Faithful in formation up the highway and into town. We parked Orv outside Eric's door and again the forty-plus friends who had helped me with the year's task joined us in celebrating with good drink and food. What a moment.

Then the sky went dark as a huge device shaded the glass door and two windows in the front of Eric's Tavern. What the heck? A moment later Jim Stromp strolled through the door. Oh-oh. He took a glass of champagne, sipped, raised it in mock tribute and again threw down a gauntlet: "Okay, Rog, you got Old Faithful and Roarin' Orv running. But I'll bet you can't get that one running," and he pointed out the door through which he had just come.

Everyone ran out the door onto the street. There, parked right in the middle of main street, right in front of Eric's, was Jim's big flatbed truck. And loaded on that bed was the most beat-up Allis WC I have ever seen in my life, encased in a wad of sheet metal that, someone told me, had once been a two-row cornpicker. Jim explained that it was a little dirty and beat-up because he had to haul it out of a wood lot where it had been sitting for twenty years or so.

My jaw dropped. "That's no cornpicker," someone laughed, picking hunks of rotten wood from its elevator and conveyors, wheels and radiator. "It's a woodpecker!" And so the wreck found its name—The Woodpecker.

Jim hauled the wreckage down to my farm after Roarin' Orv's party and dumped it behind the shop where it sat for another couple months. The first problem was getting the cornpicker off the tractor, the second, getting it into the shop.

For one thing, I had already started working on another tractor so the shop was not available, and wouldn't be for several more months. For another, I could not for the life of me figure out how to get that cornpicker off what was left of the tractor. Old farmers looked at it; they couldn't recall how they put one of those pickers on, or got it off. Two told me all they could remember was that you drove the tractor onto the picker from the back. Well, jeez, I'm utterly ignorant, but even I could see you had to back into it.

So, I stood and stared for a while. I stared for a couple months, in fact. I used a couple thousand gallons of water to wash the worst of the dirt from the

A Proper Set of Farm Tools

From Cenex, *"Partners," January 1991*

I haven't been a farmer very long, but I am a fast learner. For example, there was the time Woodrow Buehler and I were hauling firewood, and I jackknifed my trailer tongue back under the bed of my pickup truck. Woodrow stood there looking at the mess a minute, shaking his head and mumbling something about "city boys who never backed up anything in their lives except maybe a floor drain," and then he says to me, "I don't suppose you have any tools with you either."

I sensed a chance to save my dignity. I said, "Sure do. What do you need?"

"Why don't you just bring me your tools and we'll take a quick inventory of what you got and what we need."

I dug back behind the seat of the pickup, knowing that I was going to come out of this disaster a hero, because I had tools—good ones. You see, when I moved out here, I went to the store and blew $16 on a matched set of tools in a real neat red plastic box. The package consisted of two plastic handles into which fit a whole world of tool ends, all neatly arranged in little holes in the box: a Phillips and regular screwdriver, a tack-hammer head, a half-dozen socket ends, a crescent wrench head, a nail set, and a magnet, the latter apparently for fishing the other tool parts out of the well or the engine block when they fall out of the plastic handles. There were also two pre-moistened and scented napkins in tinfoil packets for wiping your hands after you've finished replacing the transmission or loading hogs.

Well, I grabbed the tools and hurried back to Woodrow, who was trying to sort out the trailer hitch from the pickup's bumper, the tongue jack from the emergency brake, and order from chaos. I proudly opened the little red box and showed him the tools. He stood aghast. "What is that?"

"My tools."

"Those aren't tools. Those look like things they give you in fancy restaurants to eat salad with. Roger, glommers are tools, and sharp things. Where's your pry bar, and your come-along, and your cheater? What we need here is not those dainty things. What we need, Roger, is tools. Like a beater. Where is your beater?"

We wound up walking nearly a mile over to Lornemeier's place to borrow his pry bar and beater, which wouldn't have bothered me, except that Woodrow made me take along the little red box of salad tools so Lornemeier could laugh at them, too. We eventually got the trailer out from under the truck, and not many days later Woodrow came driving into our yard and told me to stand still while he told me something. "If you're going to live in the country, you better do it right," he said, and he proceeded to present me with a set of authentic farm tools.

"That's your glommer," he said, handing me something that looked like a pair of worn out ice-tongs that had been redrilled and fitted with a half-inch bolt.

"What is it?" I asked.

"It's a pair of worn-out ice-tongs redrilled and fitted with a half-inch bolt," he said. "Use it for glomming onto things. And this is a beater."

"Looks for all the world like an eighteen-inch pipe wrench with the top jaws broken off and the handle bent halfway around."

"That's what it *was*. *Now* it's a beater," said Woodrow. "And this is your pointy thing." It looked for all the world like a piece of number nine wire with the end sharpened by rubbing it up against a brick, but by now I knew better than to ask.

continued on next page

"Cheater," he said, handing me a three-foot length of two-inch pipe with the threads all boogered up. The pry bar looked for all the world like an axle off a Model A, sharpened at one end and flattened at the other. He identified a complicated mess of gears, cable, and iron as a come-along—"but some folks call them 'calf-pullers.'"

"Why do they call them 'calf-pullers?'" I asked.

"Son," Woodrow said, putting his arm around my shoulder. "If you don't know why they call them 'calf-pullers,' you don't *want* to know why they call them 'calf pullers.'"

"How do I use all this stuff?"

"Believe me, when the time comes, you will know what to use and how to use it. These things weren't designed by some engineer at a tool factory or a professor at a university; they have been refined by ten thousand years of applied farming. Indians used a glommer when they were hunting buffalo and cavemen had beaters before they had the wheel."

While what Woodrow told me turned out to be true, he later confessed, "Rog, you're still too fancy. Anything you can't fix with a beater, you better drag on into town and let them hook up to a computer or something."

The only surprise came the time when I was going fishing with Woodrow and his car broke down. He opened the hood and was yanking at wires and poking at plastic things, when he said to me, "Rog, get me the crescent wrench laying on the dash."

"Crescent wrench?" I wondered to myself. "What happened to glommers and sharp things and beaters?" A little disappointed, I got the wrench and handed it to Woodrow, who anticipated my question. He held the wrench up, grinned, and said, "Beater." He again dived under the hood and proceeded to pound on something.

wreckage, adding thereby another seventeen or eighteen acres to my farm. Still I couldn't find the key to unlock the cornpicker from the tractor.

Then a little old lady came through town looking for me—I was out of town at the time—and left a couple of operating manuals for old tractors. They weren't Allises, so I wasn't much interested, but I looked through them anyway, just in case I could pick up some hints and clues. The books were for 1920's model tractors and explained how to jack up the rear end of the tractor with a couple of logs by laying one log on the ground and using the other as a lever, how to pull the engine by hoisting it from a tree limb, and showed various other scenes of earthy looking fellows banging away on a tractor with the rearend of a monkey wrench.

The next time I stared at that cornpicker, I thought about those tractor manuals and something pretty profound hit me. (Okay, maybe it's not all that profound, but for someone as slow as me, it was kinda profound.) The farmers who worked on these machines—and mounted that cornpicker—used tree branches, logs, and monkey wrenches, and that was about it. These tractors I love were probably the first machines they owned after they traded off Nell and Ned, the draft horses. You don't need socket wrenches, visegrip pliers, and breaker bars to deal with a slow Belgian mare! These guys probably owned a monkey wrench, which they used mostly as a hammer, and maybe a little stamped out wrench with six different hex sizes that came along with the cornpicker when they bought it. THIS CANNOT BE COMPLICATED!

Moreover, these guys were farmers. They couldn't take three days to mount and dismount this blasted cornpicker on their one and only tractor. THIS CANNOT BE COMPLICATED!

Besides, these machines were in their infancy, at the most primitive stages of their development. THIS CANNOT BE COMPLICATED!

Just as you have to try to think like a stuck nut when you're trying to dislodge a stuck nut, it occurred to me, standing there staring at that cornpicker, I needed to start thinking like a cornpicker—no, actually, a farmer in 1936. No time, no tools, no hoists, no help—just me, a monkey wrench, and that picker. I peered into the maze of gears, chains, sheet metal, rods, screws, bolts, nuts, and...oh yes, rotten wood, mushrooms, squirrel nests, rusty tobacco cans, and the muck of thirty years of inattention. I kept saying to myself, "Self, think like an old farmer whose only tool is a monkey wrench."

And just as clear as day, after all those days of team-staring, I spotted these two very large, square nuts. I got a 1 1/4-inch wrench (although not a monkey wrench), a two-pound machinist's hammer, and a can of penetrating oil. I basted the nuts liberally with oil, tapped them a couple times with the hammer, and applied the wrench. The nuts turned firmly but smoothly. And clunk! The cornpicker fell from the tractor, just like that.

Believe me, that little piece of advice—THIS CANNOT BE COMPLICATED—is the best I can offer you. Keep reminding yourself that the men who worked on these tractors knew less than you do, no matter how little you know, because, though this may be new to you and there is an awful lot to learn, the last bolt the original owner fastened was probably a tightener on his team's harness. If he did it, you can do it.

The next step was to move the tractor out of the cornpicker apparatus around it, which involved hooking a working tractor on the front of the wrecked tractor with a chain and dragging it close to the door of my shop.

I once visited a farm where the owners proudly showed me a treadmill that had belonged to their grandparents. The treadmill was hooked to a washing machine, so all you had to do was catch a farm dog and put him on the treadmill where he would walk uphill all day and wash your clothes. The machine worked just fine; the problem was that the family dogs quickly learned to be scarce on Mondays. (Don't ask me how they knew which days were Mondays but these good, honest folks insisted they did.) So, the dogs had to be lured into a barn stall sometime Sunday before they knew what was coming up. (Nor do I understand why the dogs could figure out Mondays but not Sundays.)

Hauling a dead tractor requires two people—one to drive the pulling tractor and a second to steer the wreck. The only two other people on this farm are my daughter Antonia and my wife Linda, both of whom would rather eat live crickets than help me tow tractors. It is my impression that I offer plenty of well-meant, clearly expressed suggestions as we are towing; they insist that I yell and scream at them, not always with polite turns of phrase. So, I caught Linda on a Sunday, when she had no idea what I had in mind, and I wrestled her over to the tractors. She finally gave in when I used my patented double-throwover wrist lock and offered to let her sit on the towed tractor rather than drive the puller.

"It's easy," I assured her as I slowly eased up on the wrist lock. "All you have to do is sit there on the Allis while I drag it over to the shop. You won't have to use the brakes or clutch or anything. Just sit there and steer."

I had to work fast, of course, because as soon as she hauled herself up on the broken wreck, surveyed the rusty seat, and grasped the black-staining steering wheel, I'd never get her back up on the machine a second time, no matter what. I quickly pulled the chain snug and began to haul the tractor out of the picker. Sheet metal screeched and the old tractor, unaccustomed to rolling, lurched and clanked. The little International 300 I was driving roared with the strain. The Allis rolled forward on its rusted, broken wheels, pitching from one side to the other, dragging, tearing rubber. The tractor bucked as the chain forced it forward. As I looked back, I could see that Linda, partially obscured by the smudge of black smoke the International was throwing back over her, was screaming something at the top of her lungs but at the time it seemed important to me to keep that tractor's momentum going, so I yelled, "Huh?" just to show her I cared, and kept on going.

A few minutes later I had the Allis pulled into position and eased back on the throttle of the International. Linda had quite a bit to say, right then, a lot of it on the personal side, so I'll skip that part, but once when she paused to catch her breath, I commented that Jim Stromp had suggested we take pictures of this project so we had a record of how it had progressed. Linda looked at me, dusting the rust off her jeans and the black rubber off her hands and the dirt from her hair and the oil from her brow, and said, just as calm as can be, "Good idea, Rog. Photos like that would stand up pretty good in divorce court."

When towing tractors, get a buddy from town to help you. It may seem like a lot of trouble at the time but, believe me, in the long run it's the easiest thing in the world.

Next I hauled the unfinished tractor I'd been working on for months out of the shop. I had reached something of a stalemate anyway. I needed to do some bodywork that involved welding and I either had to take the parts to a welding shop or learn how to weld. Since welding is a skill I could really use, I decided to delay the work on the machine I'd been working on, get some basic experience in welding over the winter, and work instead on the challenge issued by Jim Stromp. Besides, working on The Woodpecker promised to be more fun. I tucked the unfinished machine under cover, tucked a tarp over it, and promised to return in the spring.

While the shop was empty, I swept it out, cleaned some oil spots off the floor, moved heavy items like jacks, jack stands, some larger parts like radiators and axles out, and generally put everything in order while I had some extra room to move around. I cleaned off my work tables, emptied the trash buckets, and tried to get everything ready to welcome The Woodpecker to its new home for a year or so.

All four tires on The Woodpecker Allis were little more than carbonized shreds, the wheels rusty shards, so I decided to put "working wheels" on her before pulling her into the shop, and there's a story there too. Eighteen months earlier, when I was about to haul Silent Orv into the shop, I was in a little better shape in regard to tires and wheels: Orv had some pretty decent tires and wheels on the back end (although none on the front). I put the front end in a two-wheel tractor dolly—nothing but a little cart that carries the front end so a narrow-front tractor can be towed—and winched the tractor toward the shop with a come-along, a simple hand-winch. That takes time, but I'm in no hurry and at this stage, sometimes it's easier when things progress slowly.

As Orv's front end entered the shop door and the rear wheels approached, I laughed at myself because a kind of optical illusion made the rear wheels seem too wide to go through the doors. Hahahahahahaha. When my brother-in-law Steve built the shop for me, we carefully measured the width of Sweet Allis, The Giltner, and two scrap tractors, all of the same model, and they all measured about 86 inches. So, we figured it would be simple enough to hang two sheets of four-by-eight-foot plywood for the door, giving me a generous 96-inch opening, five inches to spare on each side. Hahahahahaha.

As the tractor's rear end came closer and closer to the door, the, uh, optical illusion became even more striking. In fact, when the rear wheels finally got within an inch of the doorway, it became obvious even to me that there was no way in billy-hell that thing was going to fit between the sills. Thus I learned that tractor wheels can be reversed for a narrow or wide setting and good ol'

Orv was set wide. Hey, no problem! Just take off the back wheels and turn them around, right?

So I backed off the winch a little and let Orv roll back down the shop's entry ramp a couple feet. I jacked up the rear end and blocked it. I used a big lug wrench to turn the lugs off the wheel and tugged the wheel off, intending to hold it up, spin it around, and rebolt it to the wheel, thus narrowing the tractor's beam. No dummy, me!

Thus I learned that some tractors have a liquid ballast in the back tires that results in the tire and wheel weighing about the same as the planet Saturn— something in the neighborhood of twelve trillion metric tons. Demonstrating the agility of a much younger man, I managed to get out of the way of the wheel as it fell over, registering seven on the Richter scale on earthquake measuring devices in Denver.

Now I had a tractor half in, half out of the shop, balanced on one side on a jack stand, on another liquid-filled tire on the other. The only thing I could do was leave the shop open all winter, working on the front of the tractor inside the shop, the rear end outside in the snow. Or I could take off the other tire, let it fall to the ground, hopefully not collapsing coal mines in Pennsylvania, and mount something else on the rear axle of Orv so I could somehow roll him into the shop. And that's what I did: I mounted two iron-lugged, narrow wheels on the tractor, and winched Orv through the door.

I liked that idea. No sense in having smelly, leaky, bulky tires on a tractor you're going to be working around for a year or so. Now I have a pair of iron-lug wheels but without the lugs (which can damage a shop floor) and it is my standard practice to take off whatever rear wheels are on the tractor about to be restored and install the "working wheels." (After I pulled Orv out of the shop, I tried to put the liquid-filled tires back on, but turned to narrow width in case I needed to work on him again. As it turned out, oversize tires made it impossible to mount the wheels at narrow spacing at any rate, so I would have had to take the wheels off no matter what. Small comfort.)

So, I put the working wheels on The Woodpecker, discarding the old ones as junk, which flattered them. I winched it (some tractors like Orv are male, some like Sweet Allis are female; I haven't gotten to know Woodpecker well enough yet, so it's still "it") into the shop, where I think I heard it sigh with pleasure at the idea of being cleaned, repaired, and brought back to life.

Chapter Two

The Shop ◆

*T*here are two schools of shop design (at least two): the Hospital Operating Room Approach and the Explosion in a Scrap Yard Approach. Watch one of the many television shows on car racing sometime, if you aren't

like me and wouldn't miss one anyway. Often these shows take you into a race car shop where cars are built from scratch. The floors are immaculate; the walls are bare; the workers wear uniforms without a stain. When a mechanic needs, say, a 9/16th socket, he goes to a big, red cabinet on wheels, opens the drawer marked "Sockets, SAE," and moves the needed item from a neat little rack in the drawer. When he's done with that socket, he puts it back.

Now, that sort of tidiness is expensive. Organization like that doesn't come cheap. Kenny Porath is a local auto mechanic of the technologically advanced kind. He uses computers on modern engines and has invested in a fortune's worth of top-of-the-line tools. His shop is the attached garage of his home and is about as tidy, clean, and neat as his wife Marna's kitchen, and she is a pro-

The Nebraska Triangle

From syndicated column, "Roger, Over and Out," January 1993

One of the reasons I had such a good holiday season this winter is that I made darn sure I elbowed out some "quality time" with my Allis WC tractors! I was stuck in an airport somewhere in early December when I formulated my "Christmas 1992 Fantasy." I planned to take a full week off, never opening an envelope or answering a telephone call. I was going to devote days to working on my tractors, I was going to clean my office (yeah, that may not sound like much to you, but it is a project that is usually done with a skid loader and a flame thrower!) and straighten out the attic, a job I have been avoiding since we moved into the house five years ago.

Well, none of that was to be, it turned out. There was mail I *had* to take care of, and telephone calls that *needed* answering, and other things that simply *demanded* attention. Every day I looked longingly toward my new shop, dreaming of a time when I could finally get to occupy it.

And finally that day came. But things didn't go quite the way I'd hoped.

Lovely Linda, bless her heart, gave me for Christmas one of those big, fancy, rolling, red tool boxes like *real* mechanics use. When I finally got a day off of the usual stuff, I anticipated the joy of setting up those drawers and lovingly distributing my tools in those pretty little compartments. I took the components out of their cardboard boxes. I stepped back and admired the beauty of those red jewels. I got some wrenches. I found the little cloth sack with the keys and opened the bottom drawers so I could install the wheels—actually the only assembling the tool chest needed. I put on the wheels. I put the top box on the lower box. I rolled the chest over to its place along the shop wall. Again I stepped back and admired my work and Lovely Linda's kindness.

Time to put away tools! Could anything be more fun?! It was snowing outside but I had a nice fire going in the woodstove. The radio was playing my kind of music. What fun this was going to be! I'll just unlock the top drawers and... Unlock the top drawers... Unlock... What did I do with the keys? They've got to be here somewhere. I haven't even been out of the room. They have to be right here. I can see that little cloth bag containing the keys right in front of me.

I looked for over an hour for that miserable little bag. I sifted the ashes in the stove in case I had burned it with the packing. I lifted up everything. I looked under, behind, over, through every tool, container, part, and parcel *twice*. Finally, I admitted defeat and went to the house to ask Linda and Antonia to help me. *They* looked under, behind, over, through everything. No keys. The Ladies went back to the house to call Sears to have duplicate keys made, leaving me to sit in the shop staring at that locked tool box.

One last time I decided to lift up the top box and see if maybe the keys had fallen behind it or stuck to it or welded themselves to the wall or something. Hmmm. This little top lid seems loose. In fact, the top tray is open! I guess it doesn't lock when the other drawers do. And...and in that top tray was the little bag of keys, right where I had thrown them *so I wouldn't lose them!*

fessional caterer. I was at his place one time for a barbecue party and Kenny got pretty miffed when his father-in-law accidentally spilled barbecue sauce on the shop floor. You don't spill things on the floor of Kenny Porath's shop.

Kenny's tools are packed into a huge, red, multi-drawered cabinet on wheels, the collection worth about as much as my home. When Kenny loans a tool—a rare event and one I certainly don't recommend—you sign a little slip of paper bearing a description of the purloined item and it is deposited in the empty slot where the tool usually rests. When you borrow a tool, sometimes Kenny makes you wear a bright yellow vest that says, in big, red letters, "Neither a borrower nor a lender be," and I think that's a good idea.

Remember Dale Muhlbach's shop where Dan, Mick, and I went to test magnetos for Roarin' Orv? Well, Dale's shop is a ragged, old farm building. I'd guess it was once an automobile garage but now isn't big enough to hold most modern vehicles. There are boxes of rusty bolts and nuts, cobwebs in the corners, scrap iron buckets, and tools hang on bent nails on the unpainted walls. Dale's efficiency comes from his spartan tool chest. I've only been in his shop once, the day Mick, Dan and I tested those magnetos, but I saw only one wrench, a largish crescent wrench that had once been broken off and was welded back together, a large-and a medium-size screwdriver, a mechanic's hammer (not a claw hammer, which is crucial to carpenters but not much good for mechanics), and...well, that's pretty much it. In other words, Dale's shop is a good reflection of the Spartan shops the folks who originally worked with these old tractors must have had.

Don Hochstetler is an old friend of mine and our local machinist. (He is also a well driller, mechanic, plumber, and weather forecaster.) His shop is crowded with engine parts, unidentifiable hunks of iron, machines, tools, supplies, and stock. All the drawers on his benches are pulled open and are stuffed with undifferentiated hardware—chisels, washers, drill bits, sheet metal, rasps, emery paper, jars of small parts and things that give every impression of having once been liquid. But Don knows where everything is (most of the time anyway) and feels comfortable in his shop, and he gets the job done, and that's what counts.

My shop is a combination of extremes, and it is comfortable for me. Although secretly I wish it were more like Kenny Porath's, I haven't figured out how to reach that ideal. I work hard at maintaining what order I can because I know the penalties if I don't. My shop is a small (20' x 30') tin shed with two large (8' x 8') doors, each leading into a bay just big enough to hold an Allis Chalmers WC (unless the rear wheels are set wide). I have a couple of multi-drawered tool chests, one a gift from a buddy, Mel Halsey, the other the gift from my wife Linda. They are both good ones. If you ever decide to buy a tool chest for yourself, whatever you do, don't buy a cheapie; the drawers don't open or close right, the handles fall off, and you'll find you'd rather have no tool chest at all than a cheap one. Most of my tools hang on relatively neatly placed Sheetrock screws in the walls. I need to see my tools. I grab a handful and carry them to the job. I leave them there and go grab another handful. I just can't take the time to open a drawer, take out a socket, go to the job, carry it back because it's too small, get another one, carry it back because it's too large, and finally get the right one, only to find that I accidentally grabbed an eight-point socket rather than a six-pointer. You might say I'm too dumb to be tidy, but then you also might remember that I'm a pretty big boy and don't take kindly to being called dumb. Maybe this will make the situation clear to you: my shop is a darned-sight tidier than my closet, but not as tidy as Linda's.

My shop furniture is, uh, economical. I made two work benches, one out of an old metal door, the other from some tongue-and-groove oak flooring I salvaged from an abandoned farm house. My work stool is an old bar stool I begged from my friend Eric who runs the town tavern. My welding table is a kitchenette table my mother was throwing out.

I have a car seat from a 1969 Chevy van for visitors, but since I never have visitors, it is mostly a place to pile stuff I need to take to the house or just brought to the shop from the house. I have a steel table for parts bins and supplies that I salvaged from the trash behind Harriett's Danish Cafe one day. I actually bought several brand-spanking-new utility shelves for my library. The desk on which I place my reference materials is a piece of old siding screwed to the wall. The short wall farthest away from my shop benches is covered with shelves attached directly to the wall with inexpensive brackets.

The shop is heated with a $35 wood stove (I like to say that there is no perfume like the combined aromas of gasoline fumes and a wood fire—just kidding, just kidding!) I took a lot of flak for it, but last summer I put in an air conditioner; mechanics told me I'd get a headache and that I'm a sissy, but I found that I was not spending a lot of time in the shop when I was able to work on a tractor in one bay and bake bread in the other. Without an oven. So, I have an air conditioner now and I don't care what you think.

To my mind, one of the most important features of my shop, and one that is often neglected in other shops, is the library. No kidding. I fastened an eighteen- by-thirty-inch piece of scrap plywood siding to the wall, at a level where I can easily use it while standing close to my work benches or tractor. It sits at a slight angle, has a lip to keep books, notepads, and papers from falling off, and a simple light overhead. No matter what the project, I spend a lot of time at this station. I'll tell you more about what I use in the library and how I use it when I get to the section on resources and information, okay?

My shop decor is, as they say, eclectic. I have a "Tractors with lugs prohibited" sign furnished by an old friend (and I have saved a spot for Linda's threatened parallel sign, "Lugs with tractors prohibited"). I haven't had the nerve to put up my "No Gurls" sign, especially since I keep hoping my daughter Antonia will rediscover the charm of smelling like kerosene and Goop grease remover.

I have had real trouble with good-hearted folks—not mechanics or neighbors but tourists—dropping by, saying "All I really want is to talk with you fifteen or thirty minutes." Read: "An hour or two." My shop hours are few and far between and therefore about as precious in my life as gold. Visitors may want to spend a half hour or so chatting, but I don't. We have tried to discourage droppers-in with a sign at the top of our lane saying, "KEEP OUT! NO VISITORS PLEASE," but we have found that most folks figure that doesn't mean them and there is nothing I would like better than to toss aside my wrenches, turn off my music, and hear their story about how they retired from the postal service last fall and have been crossing the country in their RV ever since, adding whenever they can to Wilma's salt and pepper shaker collection and visiting small-time television personalities like me, and have I ever been to Ottumwa, Iowa, and what's Charles Osgood really like?

We put up a sign that says, "WARNING: GUARD DOGS ON DUTY," but its effectiveness is somewhat diminished when our black lab Lucky comes running up with his frisbee, obviously eager for the unwanted visitors to throw it for him. As our UPS guy said when he first saw the sign and looked over at Lucky with his frisbee, "Hmmm, I guess he must be on break, huh?" Linda solved our problem of uninvited visitors when she found some unusual signs in Gempler's (also a great place to find repair tools and supplies for old tractor tires: for an address, see Appendix B). We put one on the shop door that reads:

DANGER
DEADLY MANURE GASES POSSIBLE
DEATH
MAY BE IMMEDIATE!
ENTER PIT ONLY WITH:
- **SELF-CONTAINED AIR SUPPLY**
- **VENTILATION**
- **RESCUE HARNESS, MECHANICAL LIFT, STAND-BY PERSON**

I was worried about the possible dishonesty of the sign but Linda assures me it is too close to the truth to be deemed anything but scrupulously honest.

Gemplers also supplied the sign we finally put on our gate that stopped the uninvited visitors problem dead in its tracks:

DANGER
THESE MONKEYS BITE AND CAUSE SERIOUS INJURIES. DO NOT APPROACH!!

I have no idea why people are more frightened by the prospect of being bitten by monkeys than three big, barking farm dogs, or why Gemplers carries these signs in its catalog, but take it from me, the monkey signs stop trespassers dead in their tracks.

My shop walls sport a couple posters and tavern signs featuring racing cars, antique tractor photos and ads, some pictures drawn by Antonia when she was much younger, photos of my favorite things—Stilton cheese and port wine, Antonia, black lab dogs, Cindy Crawford, lists of things I need to buy the next time I go to town, notes of things I need to remember—the order of the parts I took off the PTO shaft when I took it apart, the best amperage and rod type to use for welding various gauges of metal, Cindy Crawford. And over the tool racks I have a clock, a thermometer, and Cindy Crawford.

One of the most useful items I have come up with for my shop is a sheet of gray sheet metal about two by three feet, right above the stand-up desk where I keep all my shop manuals—I think it's the back off an old military desk; I have a dozen or so old magnets stuck to it and I use it to post everything from supplies I need to buy on my next trip to town to a listing of the order parts as they come out of an engine or transmission's interior. There is also a small calendar with pictures of very naughty girls, just in case I need to know exactly what day it is.

There is also a photo of Miss November from a 1992 Al's Garage calendar which I haven't been able to bring myself to throw away since I can tell by the way she's looking at me that's she's crazy about me and, probably, Allis Chalmers WCs.

In fact, arguably the single most important element of any shop, an item most shops have in common, is your mandatory naughty calendar. You can bang together your own work table; you can count on friends and family to give you some big shop requirements as gifts; but, take it from me, you must get your own shop calendar. The first year I had my shop I put "shop calendar" on my Christmas list. My mother gave me a Health Day Calendar, with

The Peanut Maxim

From syndicated column, "Roger, Over and Out," February 1995

I have been working on old tractors for a couple years now and I've learned quite a bit from books, catalogs, and mechanically inclined friends. But there's one thing not a single book, not one catalog, nary a buddy bothered to tell me and yet, as it turns out, this is probably the single most important thing anyone with a good shop should know and observe: DO NOT EAT PEANUTS IN YOUR SHOP.

I know what you're thinking: Ol' Rog's clutch must be slipping. No, I am very serious and I now have plenty of experience to draw on by way of supporting this important shop rule. Last fall I pulled a derelict Allis Chalmers WC into my shop for my winter's project. Everything on this wreck was stuck or broke, so I tore it completely down, cleaned everything, freed stuck parts, replaced worn or broken elements, drained, scraped, rubbed, scrubbed, and caressed each and every piece. And then, slowly but surely, I reversed the process and began putting the old girl back together.

Around Thanksgiving the Dannebrog grocery store began carrying peanuts for the holidays. I love peanuts (or did), especially the unsalted variety. Peanuts seemed to be just the snack for the shop; they have their own clean container and the shells were a great starter for the next day's fire in my stove.

Things started to fall apart, however, in late December when a photographer came out from *Successful Farming* to get a few shots for another of the pieces I have been doing for that magazine's Old Iron series. He wanted a shot of me standing behind the tractor I was working on. I was embarrassed, however, to find that I had accidentally (and irresponsibly) put a handful of peanuts on top of the engine, right among the valves. Jeez, I spent weeks cleaning that engine and here were the delicate valves and lifters full of peanut dust, shells, and hulls. I explained that I had probably been eating peanuts and someone came into the yard and I went out to talk with them and without thinking I put the peanuts on the engine and... Well, whatever I said didn't make much difference to the photographer, I'm sure. Some mechanic, he was probably thinking. Peanuts in the valve cover.

A few weeks later, I got to the transmission. I had removed the PTO from under it and the shifter cover from the top, so it was pretty much an open, iron box full of gears. I was about to start loosening up gears when I noticed in the bottom of the gear box—peanuts. Lots of peanuts. Handfuls of peanuts. Jeez, I thought, I must have been eating the blasted things and spilled a cup of them into the transmission. Not only was it a mess to clean out, I kept thinking of what a disaster it might have been if I had tried to run that tractor with a transmission full of peanuts.

I was chagrined, not only by my sloppiness, but by my forgetfulness in not recalling spilling them.

A couple weeks ago I got to reassembling the cooling system. I wanted to clear the mounting holes under the radiator, so I turned it over on my workbench. And out fell a good pound of peanuts. Now, I know for a fact I didn't put those peanuts into the radiator. And I didn't accidentally drop them in there either.

One gloriously warm day in January I cleaned the shop and found stashes of peanuts everywhere. I'm not sure who the culprit was—mice around here seem too small to haul whole, unshelled peanuts around, but someone—ground squirrel, mouse, whatever—has obviously been lifting my peanuts all winter and stuffing

continued on next page

them into safe places like valve covers, transmissions, and radiators. Also, parts bins, sleeve pullers, engine stands, rag boxes, spare carburetors, air cleaners, mufflers... you get the idea.

Now there is a big hand-lettered sign clearly visible as you come into my shop:

> ## NOT RESPONSIBLE FOR ACCIDENTS, AND ABSOLUTELY NO PEANUTS!

useful health tips for each day of the year—for example, "Watch your diet and wherever possible limit your fat intake," or "As the weather gets colder this month, be sure to dress appropriately," or "Maybe it's time you look for a hobby that doesn't weigh quite so much."

My wife Linda gave me a calendar that was a definite improvement, featuring a lovely lady wearing fashionable clothes, complete with sidebars of the models' favorite diet recipes. Oh, boy.

I don't care if you're a Baptist preacher, if you have a shop it is required by everything that is decent and manly to have a racy calendar on the wall. There simply is no choice. Go to your local service station or auto mechanic's workplace and take a look at the calendars there. See what I mean? No girlie calendar, no mechanic you can trust.

Most mechanics, I suppose, start with a coffee can or two for spare nuts, bolts, and washers, but inevitably we all graduate to larger bins, boxes, and buckets. I like large square or rectangular containers because they fit together more neatly on my workbench (and that's where I keep my hardware bins, on the workbench). I have a large bolt bin, small bolt bin, a washer bin, and all-Allis hardware bin. I keep new hardware separate to keep it clean and in some sort of order. I also keep a collection of various old frying pans, baking trays, and cake pans for sorting hardware from the bins when I am looking for something; that's easier than digging around in the whole bin or pouring everything out onto your workbench for inspection.

Once you get into tractor mechanic work, you will find that hardware takes on a whole new importance in your life. You will never again walk by a shiny washer or nut lying on the sidewalk. You may pass by a quarter, but not a washer. Your wife will never again do a load of laundry without finding a bolt or two in the bottom of the washer tub. Nothing gives a mechanic more comfort than bins chock-full of nuts, bolts, or washers, and that nut lying there in the gutter may be precisely the one you'll be looking for the next time you dig into the nut bin.

I knew I married the right woman when we were driving through the streets of Grand Island a couple years ago and I pulled the car up to a hasty stop. "What's wrong?" Linda asked with concern as I jammed the car into reverse and squealed back ten yards or so. "There. Right there. By the curb. It's a great big nut. I'll bet that baby is a full one-incher. We've got to go back."

Without hesitation, Linda jumped out of her side of the car, ignoring the cars honking behind us, grabbed that orphan nut, and jumped back into our vehicle. "My god," she gasped as she thought about what she'd just done and hefted the hunk of iron in her hand. "I've never seen a nut this big...except maybe for the two of us!"

"I love you, Linda Lou," I sighed.

Also on my parts and supplies shelves I have smaller paint-can buckets for pins, brass fittings, and springs, an old cookie box for old gaskets (for patterns) I can salvage and gasket patterns I have made. I am currently switching the cookie box over to rectangular plastic containers dry cat food comes in. Less wasted space on the shelves, you know? I have purchased a couple commercial collections of parts, like a box of assorted o-rings, which has been moderately useful, and a cotter key collection, which has been very useful. There are a couple cans for carburetor parts, manifold studs, and magneto parts. And a can with one, very large nut in it.

Chapter Three

Tools ◆

I like tools, and so I've bought a lot of them—a lot more than I need. Bondo, my auto body repairman pal, was once surveying my shop and picked up a box that had just been delivered by the UPS man. He shook out the strange looking pliers-device inside and looked at me quizzically. "One-handed spark plug gap adjuster," I explained.

"When they have the farm sale after you die," he said sagely (and probably correctly), "the auctioneer will hold this thing up and say, 'Here you go, boys, a one-handed spark plug gapper, still in the original box.' " I've never used it. I don't need a one-handed spark plug gapper, and you don't either.

On the other hand, sometimes gadgets sound absolutely goofy but wind up being darn near indispensable. Snap-Ups, for example. Snap-Ups are little white plastic doodads I spotted in some catalog or another and in a moment of idiocy, sent for. You take these four plastic plugs and screw them into the pan mount holes under the block when you are about to replace a block. You push the pan up over the pegs and little wings catch the pan and hold it in place. Then you screw in a couple bolts and screw out the Snap-Ups. Sounds pretty silly, right? Well, just try laying under that tractor, pushing the pan into place on the gooey gasket compound with one hand and then hold the bolt and tighten it with a wrench with the other. You will instantaneously see the wisdom of Snap-Ups.

While I do have more tools than I need, I do take a

Tools I Have Known

From Natural History, *"Science Lite," April 1994*

Thomas Carlyle, English essayist and historian, wrote early in the 19th century, "Man is a tool-using animal....without tools he is nothing, with tools he is all." French philosopher Henri Bergson wrote in the early years of this century: "Intelligence...is the faculty of making artificial objects, especially tools to make tools." American anthropologist and ultimate tool-man Tim Allen said a few months ago, "Man is the only animal to *borrow* tools."

Now comes Welsch's corollary: Man (or Woman) is not simply a tool-using animal, or a tool-making-tool-using animal, or even a tool-borrowing animal, but a tool-*loving* animal. The team of six accountants at Sears who handle my Craftsman tool account will verify that.

I'm kidding, of course. I have a set of tools I use for working on old tractors—a *modest* set of tools. Well, maybe it isn't really a *modest* set of tools. Lots of tools. Okay, most of my estate is tied up in socket wrenches.

More tools than I need? Well, actually, I don't need any tools at all. I could take my tractors up to town and let a real mechanic work on them. In fact, I don't even need the tractors, since my farm isn't much in the way of a farm. And my taste in tractors leans toward tractors that aren't much in the way of tractors. In fact, I make more money writing about tractors than sitting on them. But I *like* working on tractors, and I like tools, so I have tools.

I don't really need many tools to work on these tractors, which are each and every one of them an Allis Chalmers WC tractor, made from 1935 to 1942. Frankly, about all you need to work on a 1937 Allis Chalmers WC is a medium-size crescent wrench, a claw hammer, and a screwdriver. Two of each would be nice, but I suppose I could jam the bolt of a stuck nut with any old piece of yard iron if I had to.

The old maintenance and service manuals for WCs do call for some fancy tools like torque wrenches, bushing pullers, and feeler gauges, but most of these old machines, if they could talk, would tell you that they never in their sixty years of life felt a torque wrench, bushing puller, or feeler gauge.

Most old mechanics I know never use phrases like "foot-pounds torque" or ".019 tolerance." They tell me to turn down the oil pan bolts until the gasket puckers out a trifle, and to be sure the cylinder sleeve doesn't sit above the block more than will catch on a fingernail. "Tighten the nut finger tight," they say, "and then turn it another quarter of a turn." Or "Use an eight-inch crescent to tighten it just enough that your eyes pooch out a little."

Oh, but you should see how pretty that set of sockets looks, all in a row on that peg board. Here, try the heft on this 3/4-inch ratchet. And listen to the musical click it makes on the return pull. Take a look at this two-ton engine hoist; isn't that pretty? And when I put the load-leveler on it, pulling an engine is as easy as sucking the pimento out of a cocktail olive.

I love tools, but I have my limits, and I suspect that humanity does, too. Two things in my life have generated and agitated (in that order) those suspicions during the past couple weeks. First, I sent a note to our household insurance carrier requesting coverage for my shop and modest set of tools. The lady who handles our account wrote back, telling me I would have to list all my tools and the value of each one. I want you to imagine for a moment going to your agent to get collision coverage on your new Taurus and having that person say to you, "I'll need a list of all its parts and their value." You could get a second job and earn enough to buy another Taurus before you could put together an inventory like that! *continued on next page*

I went out to my shop and looked around my shop. Where would I start an inventory? Socket wrenches? Metric sockets? Crows-foot metric sockets? Three-eighths-inch drive crow's-foot metric sockets? Wobble-mount three-eighths-inch drive crow's-foot metric sockets? The good set from Sears that I don't like to get dirty, or the cheap set from Taiwan that is missing the 9/16ths socket (which doesn't really matter, I guess, because for some reason it never fit a 9/16ths bolt anyway)?

Inventory my tools? Lady, you must be crazy!

The second life-crisis that focused my attention on tools was when Lovely Linda asked me to install a window air conditioner in the window of her studio. Easy enough. I grabbed a hammer, a screwdriver, a tool knife (to cut plastic sealers), and a crescent wrench and headed up the stairs. I pulled the machine out of its box, pried loose the window I painted shut last summer, and got to work. As is her custom, instead of letting me get on with the job, Linda made a nuisance of herself and insisted that I waste even more time by reading the instructions.

That done, I proceeded to do what I would have done anyway. But when it came time to adjust the side curtains (never mind what side curtains are; just take my word for it that the time did come when I needed to adjust them) I found that the screws were not the good old-fashioned slotted kind, so I had to go down two flights of stairs and out to my shop to get a Phillips screwdriver. When I got back upstairs, I found that the screws weren't even Phillips head screws (the ones with the little cross on the top); these were something-else-head screws with a little star on the top. I don't know what they're called and I don't have a driver for them. I took a hacksaw and cut a groove across each one so I could use a regular screw driver. (Early in this process Linda took our daughter Antonia and fled to a safe house in a city not far from here.)

It's the same thing these days with nails, bolts, brackets, zippers, staples, knife blades, nuts, washers, whatevers. A bolt is no longer a bolt is no longer a bolt. There are Torx drivers, Allen wrenches, Pitman pullers, bastard files.

I can't say for sure but I think it all started with that jerk Phillips who invented the aberrant screwdriver. I was ready to tell him off but when I checked my dictionary I found that Henry F. Phillips died in 1958. Just as well; I wouldn't want to be around when Roger L. Welsch found out either.

As soon as Mr. Phillips worked his evil, every nut-case in the world wanted a screwdriver named after him and there went the pure and beautiful principle of a tool-box that could be carried by something less than a dump truck.

Moreover, different ethnic groups use different terms for tools. Take men and women, for example. My daughter Joyce is painting our kitchen cabinets and not ten minutes ago she came into my office and asked where she could find "a teeny-weensy sharp-end screwdriver" and "squinch-nose pliers."

Someone somewhere along the line has taken my modest fetish and degraded it into an obsession. A perversion. Even though my tractors don't *need* all those tools, all those tools need me. Now, when I cast about for the only 9/32nds-inch box-end crescent wrench I own, I can't find it. I can't find it because it is buried somewhere under all those other tools I need for installing dumb things like window air conditioners. The only solution is to buy another 9/32nds-inch box-end wrench, or maybe two, so when I can't find the second one, I can maybe find the third. And then maybe a spare I can keep in my last-resort drawer.

The natural consequence of that process is that on my next project I can't find my 7/16ths-inch ratchet wrench because it suddenly seems that all I can find is a 9/32nds-inch box-end wrench. Maybe I need a couple more 7/16th-inch ratchets. And so it goes.

particular pleasure in having the right tool for the job. It was also Bondo who early on in my mechanicking advised me not to buy cheap tools. He held up a crummy box-end/open-end combination wrench from Taiwan and said, "You'll bust this one-dollar wrench about the fourth time you use it and then you'll have the choice again of buying another one from Taiwan that will cost you a quarter every time you use it, or a really good tool for five dollars that will last you all your life, and probably your son's life too, costing not even a penny every time you use it."

I probably could have figured that out the first time I held a really good wrench. I needed a 9/16th box-end wrench and I decided to treat myself to a Craftsman professional wrench. Not just a Craftsman, which is good enough, but one of their professional wrenches which is completely polished from one beautiful end to the other. It cost a couple dollars, but hey, I'm worth it, right?

Well, the moment I held that gorgeous wrench I realized what I had been missing. I took it, a 9/16th wrench made in India, and that Taiwan job into the house. I handed Linda the Indian tool, which wouldn't even make a good paperweight. "Hold that and look at it," I said. She looked at me a little funny, but she hefted the wrench and looked at it.

Then I handed her the wrench from Taiwan, which is several steps better but still not much of a tool. She held it, looked at it.

Then I handed her the Craftsman wrench. She didn't need to hold it or look at it any longer than I had held it to realize there was absolutely no comparison. "You're telling me you want a set of these, right?" she asked.

"Right."

"Get 'em," she said. "I understand."

You'll understand, too. I'm not running a Craftsman advertisement here. There are lots of good tools out there—Snap-Ons, Macks, Stanleys. Maybe not as many good tools as bad tools, but they are there. Sure, I wish I had a set of Snap-On tools, which cost a fortune but are magnificent devices. But Craftsman is darned good—not dirt cheap, but cheaper than Snap-On and at the top of what I can afford. If I had to spend less, I'd probably go to Stanley tools. My pal Mel Halsey prefers Stanley to Craftsman (and he can't afford Snap-Ons either, which is what Kenny Porath has, although he admits that Craftsman tools are good bargains for the money). So it goes. Just don't start think-

ing you're "sav-
ing money"
by buying
junk.

Orphan Tools

In keeping
with my inclina-
tions toward sal-
vage, a lot of my
"tools" are cast-aways
I've rescued from
unlikely sources. When
I clean parts, for exam-
ple, I use really snazzy
soft plastic trays about
eighteen by twenty-four
inches, with about a one-
inch lip; they are sturdy,
durable, and easy to clean,
they keep solvent from
spilling onto my
work table. Several
visitors to my shop
have admired those
cleaning trays and
asked where I find
them. I love telling
them: when Linda

tears up the top of a plastic laundry basket, I cut off the top...and have
another of those fabulous cleaning trays.

I have a couple old tablespoons for scraping carbon from the con-
cave tops of pistons and cleaning burnt grease out of tight engine cavi-
ties. A couple broken paring knives are now shop knives, a discarded
heat lamp from the hen house is now a work light. Laundry bags, emery
boards, and shoe polishing cloths from motel rooms have now become
shop supplies. Scraps of discarded carpeting pad my work table when
I'm cleaning parts, old coffee cups hold valves, valve springs, and keepers when I'm working on a head, and Linda's discarded dishcloths and

towels become my most prized cleaning rags (not the torn sheets, old underwear, and overall legs that mop up oil and dirt and then exit the shop by way of the wood stove, but the ones I actually take back to the house to launder and use again).

My favorite tool source in terms of anecdotal value is my dentist. I hate going to the dentist. I go to the one I do because he is an antique car restorer and so we do have some things in common—and because I get tractor tools from him. I noticed in a catalog of fancy shop tools a listing for small "dental-type" tools for cleaning parts, pulling O-rings, that sort of thing. Why not the real thing, thinks I? So I made a deal with my dentist: I'll come in for regular checkups if I can have his broken, worn, or outdated tools. These have become some of the most valuable tools I have—little scrapers, nasty pointy things, hooks, scrapers, chisels. There is nothing better for cleaning tight corners in carburetors, pistons, and ignition systems than old dental tools, and my teeth have never been in better shape. (Although when I'm cleaning a piston ring groove with a dental tool, I keep wanting to say, "Okay, rinse and spit.")

To this point, the major omission in my shop's furniture is a good dog or cat. When I picture the ideal shop in my mind, I see a good ol' dog lying in the sun or maybe by the stove, a cat sleeping in the rag bin or atop the library. My shop is well outside our yard fence, and our dogs are kept inside the fence because we are close to a busy highway, so Goldie, Thud and Lucky can't get to my shop's door. Since sometimes weeks pass between times I can work in my shop, we can scarcely abandon a cat in there. The solution may be eventually to put a cat door in the wall somewhere, but then we'll have to figure out a way to keep out the possums and raccoons. Whatever the solution, I need a good dog or cat to make my shop complete.

My shop is anything but professional. I don't doubt that I am missing a lot of important tools besides a dog or cat. And I've already confessed to having a lot of things I don't need. For the most part, I accumulated things in a painfully haphazard way, taking things Dad gave me, picking up bargains at farm sales (sometimes not even knowing what I was buying), buying things that seemed like a good idea at the time, but...well, you can look for them at that auction sale, "still in the original box." What I'm going to do is grab a clipboard and notepad and just walk you through my tools, letting you know how things have worked out, or seem to be working out, or haven't worked out. Maybe my experience will save you a little trouble along the line.

I don't know if they qualify as tools or "dressing for success" but I would like to recommend a couple items of clothing right up here at the top of the list. I still feel a little silly putting on a shop apron, especially because I have never learned how to tie the damn thing behind my back and so I have to hang it from my shop press, tie the little strings, and then pull it on over my head, and when I'm wearing shorts, it looks like I'm wearing a dress, but now I can't imagine working in my shop without a shop apron. I accumulate a lot of dirt and grease when I'm in the shop and believe me, you'll be a lot more welcome coming in the back door of the house if you've taken off most of that dirt and grease when you took off your apron and hung it out in the shop. Shop aprons are cheap and sturdy and I don't find that they get in my way at all.

I have never been much of a hat or cap wearer but there is rarely a shop session when I don't tie a bandanna on my head to keep hair out of my face, sweat out of my eyes, and dirt out of everything. If nothing else, you'll need some clean kerchiefs or towels simply to wipe your face after a particularly dirty or strenuous task. (These are not the same as the shop rags I'll talk with you about below but Linda's old towels and washcloths I spoke of earlier.)

Finally, I keep several pairs of gloves on the shelf for when I'm working with particularly dirty or pointy parts. I tried rubber and plastic gloves and smear-on skin protection for when I work with solvents and oils but they just didn't work for me. They wound up getting torn and holding the chemicals against my skin even longer than would have happened otherwise. The best solvent gloves I've found are heavy-duty rubber dishwashing gloves. I hide them behind a bolt box because I have Linda convinced dishwashing gloves won't fit me. For hot things, I find that a good pair of leather welding gloves are remarkably inexpensive for what they are. I even keep a pair in our house next to the fireplace.

Little And Regular Tools

IMPORTANT WORD OF CAUTION!!!—No wife is going to suggest that you drag your engine hoist out of the shop and into the bedroom so you can help her turn the mattress. On the other hand, there is every possibility she may expect you to bring your beautiful, polished steel, extra-long, *professional grade* Craftsman 5/16ths box end wrench out of the shop and into the house to repair a cranky *toilet handle*. This is obviously out of the question.

I recommend two courses of action to prevent an unseemly, potentially even dangerous situation. First, buy your wife one of those all-in-one tools that within one handle contains all sorts of screwdrivers, a cute little crescent wrench, an awl, nail clippers, and garlic press. When she says something about the toilet handle, remind her that you got her the tool set so she could handle precisely such problems on her own, without having you mess up her bathroom. (I would not recommend, however, buying the Little Lady her very own tool kit for her birthday or your anniversary, as did my pal, the late Foon Briggs.)

Secondly, and most importantly, make it clear from the onset that tools that fit 1937 Allis Chalmers tractors, or Minnie Molines, or John Deeres, or Farmalls, or whatever, simply will not work on toilet handles, clothes dryers, or can openers any more than you can replace oleo margarine with transmission grease in a cookie recipe. Don't try to explain the situation any further than this. Just laugh, shake your head, and say something like, "Women, women, women...imagine: using a tractor wrench on a toilet handle!! She'd probably use a blender to time a magneto! Go figure!"

Take it from me, you may have a certain amount of discomfort and peril in bringing this off, but you're going to be real sorry if you don't.

I can't imagine anything more basic than a hammer. Even before I started working on tractors I had a hammer. The wrong kind, but it was a hammer. There are three hammers I use regularly in my shop: a one-pound machinist's hammer, for pounding like crazy, a brass hammer for pounding on things I don't want to bang up too badly (brass is softer than iron or steel so the hammer gets the dents instead of whatever you're pounding on), and a small tack hammer, handy for light rapping and tapping, which you do before you get mad or frustrated enough to go to the one-pound machinist's hammer.

I have on occasion brought into my shop a huge sledge hammer I use to hold my office door shut or closed, (a door-stop you can pick up and move without bending over) but those were occasions when I was really in need of busting loose something big, mostly beating a front or rear end loose from side rails. No sense in having that thing sitting around taking up room full time. I also have a rubber hammer and a hammer with a plastic composition head, which I use to rap loose stuck piston rings. And I have a black plastic no-rebound hammer; I have no idea what it's for. Maybe bodywork. Never used it.

The next most common tool found in my hand is a socket wrench ratchet. Sockets, in case you are really new to this business, are the smallish steel cups that fit snugly on bolt heads or nuts. You attach a handle to them—mostly a ratchet, which lets you crank away even in restricted spaces.

If you are going to work on old, rusty tractors, you'll definitely need a good breaker bar, a long, strong handle that fits onto sockets and gives you added leverage for bolts and nuts that are stuck, which is to say, every blasted one. The set I use most often is a half-inch drive (the square hole in the back of the sockets measures a half inch on each side); eventually you may want a 3/4-inch drive for bigger nuts and bolts and because they are much larger and therefore allow greater leverage, and because they feel so darned good in your hand. But believe me, they ain't cheap.

Eight-point sockets are for square nuts and bolts, six- and twelve-pointers for hexagonal nuts and bolts. You can probably get by without the eight-point sockets for a while. (And with a little fooling around with your twelve-point sockets, you'll discover that they will work on square nuts too! A 3/4-inch size twelve-point fits a 5/8-inch square nut or bolt head, an 11/16-inch twelve-point fits a 9/16-inch head, 7/8-inch twelve-point a 3/4-inch square, and so on. Don't tell me there isn't a God!) Sooner or later you'll be lusting for a set of "deep" sockets. These are especially long sockets so you can reach down onto long bolts—like head studs—and turn nuts too far down the shaft to reach with regular sockets.

A speed driver is a crank-type socket holder that lets you loosen or tighten nuts and bolts fast and easy, but believe me, with the kind of rusty junk you'll be working with, you won't be doing much of anything fast and easy.

There are a lot of other socket adjuncts, improvements, and doo-dads—speeders, u-joints, flex-handles, etc., and many of them are useful now and then for special problems, but the one item I bought as a doodad which turns out to be a standard piece of equipment for me is a set of extensions—plain, round rods of metal one end of which fits on a ratchet or breaker bar, the other plugging into a socket. Extensions let you reach into places where a ratchet or breaker bar won't fit, and there are lot of those on any tractor. I think my extensions are three-inch, six-inch, and nine-inch, and that seems to pretty much cover the range of what I need. I picked up a twenty-four-inch half-inch extension at a sale or junk store a long time ago and it eventually found its way into a drawer since it didn't do much more than gather dust.

I can't imagine getting along without a full set of good box-end/open-end combination wrenches. There are places where these are far better even than sockets—for example, where a socket and ratchet or breaker bar won't fit. I have my good Craftsman set, mentioned above, and then the cheapies for backup and for situations where I need one wrench to hold the nut and another to turn the bolt. Even the best of these are not outrageously expensive, so don't try to save nickels and dimes here.

I also have a set of box-end ratchet wrenches, flattish bars with holes in each end into which a bolt head or nut fits. You don't have to lift and reset these on a bolt or nut; you just keep cranking back and forth. I learned early on, from advice and experience, not to fool with those that have little levers on the side to switch from right-hand ratchet to left-hand, twist-on to twist-off. Those blasted little levers just make the tool weak and are constantly hitting some other part and reversing things for you precisely when you don't need them reversed. Take it from me, if you are going to buy a set of ratchets, get the kind you reverse by picking them up and turning them over.

While I was working on my first engine, the much loved and dearly remembered Old Faithful, every night in bed I studied the I & T tech manual (more about them later) for the Allis WC. I knew by heart, long before I got there, that the rod bearing nuts on an Allis WC engine rod cap nuts should be torqued twenty to twenty-five foot-pounds, 1/2-inch head stud nuts to seventy foot-pounds, 3/8-inch head stud nuts to twenty-five foot-pounds. All of which made it pretty clear that I needed a torque wrench for my shop. (A torque wrench measures how much force you are putting on a nut or bolt so several nuts can be tightened to the same tension or a standard, engineered tension. I have no idea what foot-pounds are, but that's what mine measures, and I do what I'm told, being a German and all.)

I told my Dad, a passionate auction sale customer, to keep an eye open for a torque wrench for me. "Why?" he asked.

"So I can tighten down the nuts and bolts on my Allis engine to prescribed tensions."

"How many guys who worked on that engine on the farm, do you suppose, had a torque wrench?" he asked.

Good question, Dad! I suppose it is best to meet factory recommendations on such things but believe me, you will quickly learn that the tolerance of these old machines for more casual standards (or, for that matter, downright slovenliness) is absolutely remarkable. I once torqued down an engine's rod caps to specs (that's the way I talk now that I'm a mechanic) and I couldn't even turn the engine over. I added the appropriate shims. Still nothing. Finally I just loosened everything up a touch. Thing ran like charm. I have a torque wrench, and I use it, but I suspect you could probably get along without one. In fact, if you are planning to work on one engine as your lifetime project, you'll only be torquing a couple dozen nuts and bolts through the whole process. Why not get as much done as possible, designate a day Torque Day, rent a torque wrench, and save yourself a bundle of bucks?

I bought an inexpensive set of crows-foot heads for my socket set— they let you work straight down on a bolt or nut, but I have yet to use them. Wasted money for me. On the other hand, I bought a couple of spark plug sockets and I use them often. (They're pretty much like regular sockets except much deeper so they fit into the plug recess and down over the top of the plug.) It's not often that I have need for an allen wrench but of course when I need one, there's no real substitute. A compact set of allen wrenches in a single jackknife handle is not expensive, so sometime when you're in a hardware store and spot a set on sale, what the heck.

I recommend having at least an X-type lug wrench—you know, the cross-armed type of the regular size you use for automobiles, but if you're going to be in this business for very long or very seriously, consider getting a larger, truck-size lug wrench, too. You'll need it for the large lug nuts on back wheels but I also use mine for larger nuts on other parts of the tractor. Those double handles can give you a lot of handy extra leverage. Since you are liable to be using "cheaters"—pieces of pipes to extend the length of wrenches and levers—think about getting good lug wrenches, and when it comes to old tractors that have been sitting in the rain and snow for a couple decades, you're going to lean on them, all right. There's a lot of pressure on those babies when you're really leaning on them.

A large pipe wrench, the standard kind used by plumbers, is very useful in turning stuck shafts, nuts, and hub caps. In fact, I don't know how to get hub caps off an Allis front wheel without a pipe wrench. If there is another tool for this job, I don't know what it is, but it seems to me that a pipe wrench is useful anyway, and it sure works on those big hub caps.

Often, when I am in a situation where I need something to hold the nut steady while I turn a bolt, I use locking pliers like Visegrips. There are a lot of cheap and painfully inferior models in this category, and you'll hate yourself if you pick up one of them. This is one of those cases where having a bum tool is almost as bad as having none, sometimes worse. There are long-nose Visegrips, round-jaw, square-jaw, on and on. I have two square, two round, and one long-nose and that's plenty. ("Visegrips" is a specific brand name. In fact, those wonders were invented and are still manufacturered not far from where I live, in Nebraska. I know you're not supposed to use a specific brand name in a general sort of way, and I'm not. When I say you should have Visegrips, I think you should have Visegrips. You know by now that I like Craftsman tools, but even a Craftsman locking wrench isn't up to real Visegrips pliers.)

I never use regular household pliers. Maybe that's just one of my peculiarities but I find them clumsy and they damage parts too easily. Some amateurs (I use that word in its most positive, original meaning—"lover") swear by slip-joint pliers but I sure haven't heard much flattering about any kind of pliers from any kind of serious mechanics. I do use needle-nose pliers frequently, mostly to pull cotter pins.

If you're going to get serious about this tractor thing, you might want to consider a single-cam or, better yet, multi-cam stud puller. Engine studs, especially on the manifold but even on the head, are prone to getting good and stuck, even burned into their holes in the block or head. Even a Visegrip won't hold on strong enough to let you turn them out. Stud wrenches, which look more or less like deep-well sockets and use a ratchet or breaker bar handle, have little off-center cams in them that bear down as you apply pressure against the stud. They really clamp on and if a stud can be broken loose (or simply broken), a stud puller will do the job. The multi-cam variety can get pretty expensive but I use mine often enough that I feel they are worth the investment. Even a Craftsman single-cam stud puller is not a high-ticket item if you have a couple engines to work on. Single-cam pullers are good but not as good as the three-cammers, and not as expensive.

I've wound up using my big screwdriver more often as a pry bar or dirt scraper than a screwdriver. Allises just don't seem to have many screws on them. And glory be, no Phillips screws, ever! Since you need a large screwdriver and a medium one and that's about it, you might as well buy a couple of good ones of those too. Tell your wife I said so.

I keep a drawer in my tool chest labeled "points" and another "edges." In "points" I have chisels—all you'll really need is one large and one small, a couple center punches and pin punches, a set of hollow-point gasket hole cutters (which you'll probably never need but since I have one, I use it), an ice pick, and a couple lengths of 3/8th-inch brass rod, which I use a lot for tapping out parts I don't want to bung up with a steel punch. You could probably get by for a while, maybe forever, with some big nails for pin aligners and punches.

Under "edges" I have scrapers for cleaning off dirt and old gaskets (I prefer plain old putty knives on which I put a sharp edge with a bench grinder) and knives (mostly old kitchen knives but I also have a couple tool knives with very sharp, short blades, and a matting knife like you used to use to make model airplanes). I grab every plastic car window scraper offered me for scraping and cleaning off dirt and grease. They work fine for that long after they're no longer good for ice and snow.

For cutting off old bolts and pins, I have a good hacksaw and plenty of blades, side cutters for cutting wire and cotter pins, and, although it may be overkill, a thirty-inch bolt cutter. I don't use it very often but when I do, I am grateful I have it and can't imagine what I would have done without it. A very useful cutting tool is a nut cutter, a funny looking device that looks a bit like a nutcracker, which, of course, it is. You place the open part of the cutter over a nut and turn down the screw, which has a sharp end on it. The sharp, hard-steel blade cuts into the bolt, usually popping it open before the threads on the bolt or stud are damaged. Sure, you lose the nut, but that's a small price to pay.

I recommend a large and small file for taking the burrs off parts and smoothing down rough castings and welds, a couple funnels for pouring everything from water to old oil into jugs, a hand mirror and a little mirror on a long handle, a small magnet on a long, telescoping handle (for retrieving small parts from even smaller holes where they always seem to go if they have a choice), a flashlight for looking into those little holes for the little parts, and a couple metal rulers. I don't know what they call them—maybe "small parts retriever" or "three-finger glommer"—but one of those long things with a little plunger on the top and three little hooked fingers on the bottom is indispensable for retrieving parts dropped into the interior of the brake, engine, or transmission housing, and I am always dropping things that go down little holes. It's a talent. I don't know how often I've had to resort to this nameless little device but I love it every time.

A feeler gauge, a little book of thin metal strips of varying thicknesses, is essential but cheap. (It's used to measure gaps—for example, the clearance between the end of the valve stems and the rocker arm, which for an Allis WC is .002–.003, so you need something with which to measure.) I often use a regular, metal carpenter's tape measure, for rough measurements, when I can find it.

A tap and die set—tools for cutting threads in a hole (tap) or on a rod (die)—may not be important to you; it's easy enough to go to a machine shop to have such fairly pedestrian work done—pedestrian for a mechanic or machinist, at any rate. I do think a "chase" set is important, however. A chase doesn't cut new threads; it cleans up old ones, clearing away dirt and burrs and realigning threads. When you pull a stud from a block, it just isn't a good idea to twist that ugly piece of iron back into the same jagged hole. Take a chase, clean up the threads on the stud and the hole in the block, put on a touch of grease, and your work will be considerably easier and a lot prettier. Most chases look like regular nuts with a slightly too-large hole. (In fact, I have on occasion lost a chase in my nut bin!)

I recently got an adjustable chase from Griot's Garage (listed in Appendix B below) that fits a wide range of bolt sizes and does a great job of cleaning up lightly damaged threads, but a good set of chases is cheap enough for even a modestly equipped mechanic to afford.

I can't imagine trying to do any engine work at all without a 3/8" (good) or 1/2" (better) variable speed, reversible electric drill. They not only drill holes but turn wire brush wheels and cleaning pads and burr grinders and cylinder glaze breakers, and...well, you get the idea.

I have a small, light-duty cordless drill, also reversible, but I don't use it for tractor work. It is useful when doing carpentry work around the shop—for example, driving sheet rock screws, building book shelves, that sort of light work. You'll want a good set of bits, of course, but while you're at it, pick up a set of left-hand bits that let you drill a hole while the drill runs in reverse. This means that you can drill down the center of a stuck or broken-off bolt while the drill is turning counter clockwise, the direction that will remove the bolt. I've never been that lucky but I have been told by experienced mechanics that sometimes a left-hand bit will put enough heat and torque on a stuck bolt or stud to turn it out without further efforts.

Along that same line, I'll have to admit that I am utterly baffled by devices called bolt extractors or EZ-Outs, a trade name. The theory is that you drill a hole down the center of the stuck bolt, turn this coarsely threaded, right-hand threaded device into the hole and twist the problem bolt right out. Yeah, right. I have tried to use these blasted things several dozen times, never successfully. In fact, on three occasions I have had the extractor break off inside the stuck bolt, which creates a real problem since the extractor is made of extremely hard steel. Now you're talking about a job for a real mechanic. No fun at all. I'd rather use a left-hand bit to drill the broken or stuck bolt pretty much out and

The Bubba Ring
From Natural History, "Science Lite," April 1993

It was the day that you skipped class thirty years ago to have coffee and a doughnut with that cute sophomore in Intro to Anthro. I didn't have a chance with her, even with a chocolate doughnut, so I went to class. And that was the day Cro-Magnon Christensen bored us with his lecture about Bronislaw Malinowski's study of the Trobriand Islanders' Kula Ring. The Trobriand Islanders—get this!—trade red-shell necklaces clockwise around the Pacific islands and white-shell arm bands counterclockwise along the same route. The goal is to accumulate more and more arm bands and necklaces and thus more and more prestige, the shell jewelry having no other value *but* prestige. I can't recall what Malinowski concluded, but C-M Christensen used it as an example of how different arbitrary human behavior can be from one culture to another.

He was wrong. In the intervening years I have been struck again and again how much alike we are—us and them, Americans and less reasonable people, penny stock shufflers and Kula Ring runners. Malinowski could have saved a lot of trouble and transportation costs by coming to Nebraska. This realization came to me after a long period of serious observation, which pretty much lets Malinowski off the hook, since he didn't spend a lot of time in Nebraska. Here it's not the Kula Ring but the Bubba Ring, the big difference being that the Bubba Ring involves not worthless shells but objects of real value. Otherwise the object of the two social systems is pretty much the same: do unto others before they do unto you.

Woodrow Buehler and I were at an auction sale last week when a six-foot iron pry bar went on the block. Woodrow is constantly borrowing my pry bar because in his business—plumbing and salvage—a pry bar is the sort of thing you need every day. That means Woodrow borrows my pry bar on a regular basis. Then I go over to his place and get it back, and then he comes here and borrows it, and so on.

The pry bar at the auction drew an initial bid of twenty-five cents from Stan Kowalski, who opens every bid with an offer of twenty-five cents, whether the object in question is a mint 1957 Chevy hard top with 12,000 actual miles on it or a five-gallon bucket of used firecrackers. This time the bid stuck at a quarter for a full minute while the auctioneer begged for a dollar. "Fifty cents," Carl Kohl yelled. Another long pause.

I poked Woodrow. "That thing is going to bring less than two bucks." No reaction.

"Buck!" muttered Stan. Woodrow rocked on his heels.

"Woodrow, what are you waiting for?" He looked at me as if I had just suggested he slash his wrists or go back to school.

"Buck-fifty!" crowed Carl.

"Going, going, going…GONE! Buck fifty to Carl Kohl."

I sputtered to Woodrow, "You could have had that bar for the price of a beer."

"Why…" he paused. "*Why* would *I* buy a pry bar when *you* already own a pry bar?!"

BUBBA RING RULE #1: There is no need for two people each to own something like a pry bar.

I understand borrowing a six-foot iron pry bar: It just sits in my shed until Woodrow comes by to pick it up again, but the issue isn't always that clear. For example, Woodrow owns a canoe, but he doesn't own paddles. Paddles, to my mind, are an integral part of a canoe. Would you have a rod and reel and borrow fishing line? A road and borrow gravel? No, but in the Bubba Ring, this is a common logic.

I once showed Woodrow and our mutual buddy Lunchbox a filter I had installed in our water line. As water comes from our well, it passes through the filter, which removes ugly-bugglies, if you can excuse the technical terminology. Our water tastes fine, is healthful, and no longer requires chewing. Since Lunchbox has the same problems with his water, I thought he would be interested in the filter, and since Woodrow is a plumber, I thought it might strike his fancy too.

Lunchbox was interested; Woodrow was fascinated. "That thing is fantastic," Woodrow enthused. "Lunchbox, you ought to borrow it."

Woodrow had just proposed that I loan out part of our plumbing. I was flabbergasted. When I regained my composure, I explained, "Woodrow, you're dense as a lug nut!" Woodrow and Lunchbox were both shocked by my small-mindedness.

BUBBA RING RULE #2: Nothing is beyond borrowing.

My arrival in Dannebrog twenty years ago generated some comment—for example, "What a doofus!" Thing is, I listened to my father, who says to this day, "Never borrow anything, and when you do, return it in better condition than when you got it." I love my dad but he doesn't know zip about the Bubba Ring.

Slick once asked me to come up to his house and help him trim some trees hanging over his garage. "Sure," I said.

"Bring along your saws," Slick said. "And your ladders. And your tractor. And ropes and chains."

Uh-oh—the Bubba Ring! I thought, however, that I might avoid the inevitable complications of the Bubba Ring Syndrome by not letting my tools out of my sight, so I went up to Slick's and offered to help. That way, when we finished the job, I'd just bring my stuff home with me. Such innocence! When I left Slick's place, I was lucky to have my tractor and pants. He wound up with the ladder, ropes and chains, and saw, which I did not see again for three years.

The only reason I ever got any of my tools back is that Slick moved. Friends offered to help him but he smiled with total self-confidence and said that he wouldn't need help. All he had to do was tell everyone to come get the stuff he had borrowed over the past twenty years and he could move what was left in a cardboard box.

BUBBA RING RULE #3: You can save yourself the trouble of returning things in good condition by not returning them at all.

Slick did what he said he was going to do. I got my saw, chains, ropes, and ladder and a lot of other stuff I had almost forgotten. A week later, Slick asked me to come up and help him trim some trees that were rubbing the shingles of his new house. I said I was busy, but it didn't work. "Okay, Woodrow and I will come over and pick the stuff up. Bet you don't even have it out of your pickup truck yet."

I didn't. When I mumbled that I hadn't had my tools long enough to get reacquainted with them, even Slick had to agree. "Hmmm," he said disapprovingly. "I was hoping you would replace the bad rope on your block-and-tackle and sharpen the chain on the saw."

BUBBA RING RULE #4: Possession may be nine parts of the law, but the tenth part, repair and replacement, is the owner's responsibility.

And what's that stuff about "our block-and-tackle," "our" saw?!

BUBBA RING RULE #5: If you had trouble with the community property ruling in your recent divorce, don't even *think* about getting involved in the Bubba Ring!

Last week I witnessed a raging argument between Slick and Russell Barker. When Slick got married a few years ago, he borrowed Russell's good shoes and never got

continued on next page

around to returning them. "You stupid, no-good, irresponsible deadbeat!" Russell roared into Slick's face. "I want my shoes back, and my bowling ball, and bicycle, and hedge trimmer."

I expected fury but Slick was neither angry nor hurt. He was indignant. Russell was violating the rules of the Bubba Ring. "No matter how nasty you get, Russell," he said, "You're *not* going to make me mad enough to give your stuff back to you."

BUBBA RING RULE #6: The customer is always right.

As in the Trobriand Islands, Bubba Ring exchanges are a matter of prestige and strategy, not value and commerce, and I haven't lived out here for five years without learning a little about how things are done. This morning, for example, Woodrow stood in our farmyard kicking gravel and sucking his coffee, finally asking, "You still got the posthole digger I saw in your shed last summer?"

"Uh, I loaned it to Kenny Price when he was building fence this spring." I pawed casually through the rubble in the box of Woodrow's pickup.

"Isn't that the handle I see over there in the corner of the shed?" he said, trying to draw my attention away from his white arm-band shells.

"Well, look at this! Here's my torque wrench," I said, trying to divert his gaze from my red necklace shells.

"By golly, that *is* your posthole digger!" He moved toward the shed. Should I defend my territory or launch a threat against his? I tried both: "Hey, Woodrow, I need to borrow this set of sockets wrenches of yours for a couple days," and I moved briskly toward the shed to head off his shopping expedition.

"Yep, here it is—the posthole digger, and a minnow trap! I'm setting catfish lines tonight. I'll bring you fish by morning, wait and see!"

"Uh, Woodrow, I need the furniture dolly you borrowed two years ago."

"Why?"

"We're moving the fridge."

"Did you get a new fridge?"

"Uh, why?"

"I was thinking maybe I could borrow your old one for a bait cooler."

"Well, I am going to, uh, put the old one in my shop...and besides, I need my rake back because, er, after we redecorate the kitchen, we're starting on the lawn."

"Look at this! A tiling spade! Just what I need for..." I was losing ground.

BUBBA RING RULE #7: A beginner always loses ground.

Eventually I suspected I was being watched. I'd buy a wheelbarrow in Rising City and two days later, there was Slick, wanting to borrow a wheelbarrow. I'd buy a rasp, and the next day Woodrow needed a rasp. I couldn't wear the labels off of new tools if I waited more than three days to use them.

I learned later that Woodrow's wife's cousin Faye, Slick's daughter-in-law, works at the bank and in casual conversations with her favorite cousin she'd drop nuggets of information like, "Gosh, Bernice, the girl next to me, was, like clearing checks yesterday, and she goes, 'Here's a check from that Welsch guy, and he paid, get this, fifty smackers for a wheelbarrow!'"

BUBBA RING RULE #8: There's no hiding place.

This, obviously, is research in progress. It may always be research in progress.

(Postscript: I did finally locate my furniture dolly. Woodrow lent it to Kenny, who lent it to Slick, who lent it to his mother, who lent it to Reverend Miller, who lent it to Dave Calvin, from whom, it turned out, I had borrowed it originally twenty years ago. I'll probably never get it back, now.)

then pick the pieces of the old threads out with a small pick or—aha!—a dental tool! Forget EZ-Outs.

While we're talking about getting stuck parts apart, next time you're in a major automotive tool store, take a look at pullers. There are more kinds of pullers than you've ever imagined. Some use bolts to push wedges between seals or gears, some clamp hooked arms under a gear while a big screw is turned in the center, applying enormous pressure against a shaft to pull the gear, or seal, or bearing off. Some hook onto the item being pulled while little slide weights are hammered outward to pound the part loose. Sleeve pullers force the cylinder walls (of those tractors that have sleeves) up from the block with tremendous force.

Eventually you'll probably want a general service two-arm or three-arm puller, maybe a bar or center-bolt-type puller. This is another one of those things that seems like an extravagance (even though they are not all that expensive) until you find yourself in a situation where you really need it. (Of course, then you will probably also find that the puller you have, or the half dozen pullers you have, are not quite what you need anyway. This is one of those mysteries of life we'll never figure out—like Linda's Law: "The soundest two hours of sleep begin exactly one hour before the alarm goes off.") You could spend all your shop money on pullers and still have nothing. Look around, assess your needs, talk with mechanics.

And now we're really getting down the bits and pieces of small tools—a broom for the shop and a brush to clean off the bench, small wire brushes for cleaning parts (old toothbrushes are super for this task), larger ones for larger jobs, engine brushes for cleaning out all the little holes in an engine block, pipe cleaners for the tiny holes in carburetors, pry bars for pulling things loose from heads to carbs, a variety of chains—long, short, heavy, light—some shop tarps to put under dirty jobs (I use old sheets), work lights (I have the old-fashioned, incandescent bulb type on a long cord—but I like the kind that has a plug end near the bulb, which gives you an extra extension cord right where you need it, and I use extra-heavy-duty shop bulbs because I drop the blasted thing and drip fluids on it with depressing regularity, and a fancy-shmancy quartz lamp on an adjustable stand I can adjust any way I want), and a small, light-duty propane torch. For years I heated up stuck parts and soldered with a propane torch and did just fine. I'm now learning to weld and use a carbon arc torch for some heating jobs.

Special Tools

There are worlds of specialized tools—take a look at a catalog if you don't believe me—you may or may not eventually want. For example, sooner or later you'll need a piston ring spreader and ring compressor, but maybe you can borrow one from a friend; you'll only need one a few times in your tractor work career and then only for a few minutes. And when you're working on pistons, you may want a piston groove cleaner, but old-timers recommend using a piece of a broken piston ring for that job. (Where will you find a broken piston ring? Oh, believe me, you'll find a broken piston ring before long...right there in your hand!) A valve seat dresser is cheap enough and easy to find, so don't bother to get one until you actually need it. This is another of those tools that isn't used often or long, so you have a good chance of finding a friend who bought one, used it once, eight years ago, and tucked it into a drawer in his garage. "Want it? You can have it."

And you'll need to knock down the little ridge at the top of the cylinder where the piston stop, and reversed direction ten trillion times over its lifetime—and that requires a ridge reamer. Nothing else will do the job. Again, if you are planning to rebuild one tractor in your life, borrow a ridge reamer when you get to the point where you need it, or take your sleeves to an auto shop and have them reamed professionally; if you are going to do five or six tractors, get a ridge reamer and save yourself the mileage and grief of borrowing or paying. And once you get a ridge reamer of your own, don't loan it out if you ever hope to see it again.

I feel a little more passionately about valve spring compressors. Valves are held in place in the head of my Allis WCs (and most other old tractors) by strong, stout little springs. Little wedges called "keepers" hold the valve in the spring, and the pressure of the spring holds the keepers in place. The unit is essentially a delicately balanced time bomb. To remove a valve, you have to compress the spring, pick out the keepers, and ease the spring gently back up. The first three engines I worked on I used a small pry bar hooked under the rocker arm assembly to put pressure on the edge of the spring and force it down. I held it precariously in that position with one hand while I leaned over the valve stem and tried to fish the keepers out with a small magnet. Then I used both hands to release the spring without letting it ricochet like a stray bullet around the shop. The process was a trifle clumsy but what the heck, even if I worked on thirty engine heads in my life, would it really be worth the $30–40 a real spring compressor would cost me when my pry bar system cost me nothing?

This worked fine until one evening when I was leaning over a head resting on my shop bench, holding down a valve spring with that pry bar, removing keepers. It happened too fast for me to know exactly what happened, but the pry bar slipped off the spring, the keepers flew out, and the spring flew straight up with tremendous force and unerring accuracy right to the middle of my forehead. It was bad enough that my glasses flew off but even worse was that there was a pitch-black grease circle right smack in the middle of my forehead that resisted all efforts to remove it with any number of grease removers from Go-Jo, Gunk, and Goop to Pink Stuff, Green Stuff, and Lava soap.

My next birthday I asked for a valve spring compressor; my daughter Joyce gave me one, and every time I use it, I send up a prayer of thanks for it. And I feel a funny little pain right in the middle of my forehead.

Big Stuff

Again I'll start with those things I consider most important (if not indispensable) and move on down to what may seem like luxuries to some, maybe to most, amateur restorers.

You can't have a shop, it should be obvious, without a good, large vise on your bench. This won't be cheap—you shouldn't settle for a cheap vise—unless you're lucky enough to pick one up at an auction sale, but you can't do without. One smart thing I did with mine was to cut some thick aluminum pads that I bolted on right over the replaceable, cross-hatched iron holders that came with it. The aluminum is relatively soft and prevents the vise from marking up engine parts I secure in it. I think you can buy these things too, but they were easy to fabricate, even by a klutz like me.

I don't have an anvil, although some mechanics couldn't work without one; I use the back end of the bench vise, or any one of a couple big pieces of iron I have around the shop, or the front pedestal from whatever tractor I'm working on that moment. I suppose that's pretty sloppy, but as rarely as I have to pound on something that might require an anvil, the thing would mostly be just something else for me to kick when I am walking from one bay to the other. I have never gotten into bodywork, but I do have a set of sheet metal hammers and "dollies" (little hand-held anvils that are held behind the sheet metal being worked with the hammer) when I do find myself having to work on dents and tears in what little sheet metal there is on my Allis WCs. They don't do me much good, I'll have to admit. The sheet metal on old tractors is not like the tin foil on your car. This stuff is substantial and not easily tweaked into shape. It takes some muscle, and something more than auto body tools.

If you are going to pull your tractor into your shop (and again I can't imagine trying to work on a machine without having it in the shop), think about installing a good, strong, stout anchor in the front center of the shop floor. I have one in each bay and a heavy-duty electric winch (a gift from a friend) I can move from one to the other. If I roughly center a tractor within thirty feet of my shop, which isn't much of a job, I can then hook it to the winch and gently pull (or drag) the tractor right on in. This could be done with a manual cable winch, often called a come-along, which is the way I handled the process for years, but I sure wouldn't want to go back to that system now that I can just push a button and get the job done.

Cheap come-alongs are not only short-lived and prone to break down, they can be downright dangerous. I suggest that you go to a high-grade tool store like Sears and buy a good one.

Same with jacks. I have and use a high-rise, general purpose, farm jack for some jobs but it has a lot of disadvantages: for example, it has a very small base, which makes it prone to tipping and sinking into soft ground, sometimes pitching a tractor dangerously over to the side several feet. Because of the high elevator bar on these jacks (which allows them to go very high—too high for my taste or anyone's safety), the top can move and crush, scratch, dent, and bend not only sheet metal work but even cast-iron parts and framing members on a tractor. Or for that matter, the mechanic.

I have a hydraulic floor jack like the kind you see in service stations, and I like it because it is stable, coming up from under the machine as it does rather than hooking onto higher parts, often from a side so that the tractor has a tendency to pitch to the other side. Finally, I have a couple smaller bottle jacks I use for lifting short distances, but mostly for applying pressure against stuck pistons or sleeves. I never work on the tractor while it is on jacks. I have four stout, adjustable, commercial jack stands easily capable of holding up the entire tractor from the floor steadily. I have two extremely large, heavy, nonadjustable stands made for me by a friend who is an expert welder. I don't use these often, but I know I have them when I need them. And tucked away under my workbench are twenty or thirty lengths (from eighteen to thirty-six inches) of six-by-six and six-by-eight dimension lumber I use to chock up jack stands, or whole tractors, or engine blocks, or rear ends, or front ends. Consult with an experienced mechanic on how to arrange such shoring so it is maximally stable and strong. I don't trust concrete blocks at all for this task, although I have seen some mechanics using them, often with the concrete block on the bottom, a piece of dimension lumber distributing the weight on top of the block. You don't want to crawl under a tractor unless you are absolutely sure that baby isn't going to come down on you. Even small machines like my Allis WCs weigh a ton and a half, and that's a lot of iron.

I have three different kinds of hoists in my little shop, which may seem like a lot but they are there for very different uses and locations. Tacked onto my shop is an open-sided, dirt floor lean-to where I like to work during pleasant days, especially when I am completely disassembling a tractor for parts. If I drag a tractor into the shop to dismantle, it'll be only a matter of days before I have to start hauling engines, transmissions, wheels, frames, that sort of thing, back out. If I can take the thing apart in the open air, it's easy to bring in my International tractor's bucket so I can drag everything off where I can store it safely and less obtrusively out of the way. For that outdoor bay I had a local welder put together a swinging overhead beam; a friend in town gave me a wheeled trolley to put on the beam, and to it I fastened a chain hoist. That lets me lift an engine or transmission or fluid-filled wheel—even a whole tractor front—and move it just about anywhere I want within the bay. Now, I wish I had something like that inside the shop!

But I don't. Inside the shop I have a dolly-type engine hoist like a little crane on wheels. It has an arm that extends in length (thereby, however, diminishing its lifting capacity) and a hydraulic cylinder to raise that arm. It is on wheels so I can lift an engine from a tractor frame and move it elsewhere in the shop, or out the door where I can drop it into a tractor bucket or pickup truck bed to be taken somewhere else. I like this hoist because its long, lower legs can be removed and tucked alongside the vertical member for storage, so even though this is a very large piece of equipment, it takes up only a two-by-three-foot floor space when I'm not using it, and in a little shop like mine, space is important.

In case you're interested, my outdoor beam-hoist made by the local welder cost me about $500; the portable, commercially manufactured floor hoist about $300. Yeah, that's expensive, but it's not easy to remove an engine or transmission without one. As I have recommended before, if you are going to work on one tractor and that's it, it would be far cheaper to rent an engine hoist (or "cherry picker" as mechanics around here call them) for the little bit of time you'll need it. My pal Kenny Porath is a professional mechanic but, he reasons, engine hoists are so expensive and bulky and are used so rarely, he'd rather rent one on those rare occasions when he needs it.

Of course the old style of hoisting an engine was to fasten a block and tackle or chain hoist to a ceiling beam or overhead tree branch (there's a reason they call us "shade-tree mechanics," after all!). If you take that route, be darned sure that beam or branch will carry the weight safely. It won't take much to reinforce that beam or branch so it will be plenty safe...and maybe save your life. The Allis Chalmers WCs I work on weigh a total of 3,000 pounds, so a total engine weighs maybe 300 pounds. I have no trouble picking up a block myself and I'm no "power lifter," so we're not talking about a lot of weight here, but those 300 hard pounds dropping six feet can make quite a dent on your toes, so better safe than sorry, right?

Important adjuncts to a hoist are chains and nylon slings that can be attached to an engine or part or tied around it so it can be lifted with the hoist. When you're pulling an engine or transmission or front end off a tractor, you sometimes have to tip it a little this way or that or turn it slightly (or all the way around) to get it out from its tight home. Real joys for such jobs are a chain sling with a swivel, so the engine or part can be turned, and a leveler, a kind of balance bar with a little crank on it that lets you ever so slightly tip the engine one way or the other. These devices also let you change the orientation of a large part so you can more easily fasten it to an engine stand, if that's your intent.

On your workbench you'll want a grinder. Mine is a medium-size unit that cost about $50 new. It has a carborundum wheel for sharpening tools and taking burrs off work and a wire wheel I use for cleaning parts like valves and pistons. I have a couple ordinary window box fans I use for moving heat around the shop when it's cold and airing the place out when I've been doing something particularly smelly (like cleaning parts with solvent), dirty (blowing the dirt out of an engine), or smokey (welding).

Home-Spun Innovations

The most useful thing I have in my shop is, as far as I know, my own invention. The moment I started taking parts off that first tractor, Old Faithful nee The Giltner, I knew I had to figure out some way to keep those parts sorted out and retrievable. I put small parts in plastic bags labeled with whatever was inside—"manifold studs," "sheet metal screws," "water pump parts..." and dropped them into a large, cardboard box.

I put up a sheet of cheap, white plywood siding on a spare piece of wall and drove three-inch Sheet-rock screws into it as I took off larger parts like the air cleaner, magneto, gas tank, and that sort of thing. When I got the point where I started to put things back together, I could see what worked and what didn't. Sorting through that box of oily, dirty plastic bags was a mess. They tore and opened up, got dirty enough that I couldn't read my labeling, and every search for parts was a frustration I didn't need.

On the other hand, the parts I had hung on the wall board were readily available, easily seen against the white board, and instantly identifiable. So, now I bag and hang all my small parts on that board as I take them off. (Hint: write your identification on the plastic bags with a heavy-duty magic marker before you put the parts in them!) Larger parts, like the air cleaner or carb, I hang directly on the Sheet-rock screws. Very large parts like the radiator, hood, and wheels I roll outside the shop until I am ready to work with them. What I don't need is more clutter.

For a long time, when I needed to work under my tractor—dropping an oil pan, adjusting a clutch, draining a transmission—I had an old couch cushion I threw on the floor and lay on it. That worked fine. Eventually, however, I got a creeper, one of those low, wheeled carts you can roll around on under a car...or tractor. I bought a cheap wood one with four wheels that had the nasty habit of popping up and hitting me on the back of the head if I wasn't careful when I laid down on it or got up. I'm a big boy—about 270 pounds—and this wooden creeper made noises not unlike the sound of the Titanic as it was going down—not a sound I want to hear in my life.

Eventually I got tired of the lumps on my bean and a growing fear of icebergs and bought a really nice, tough, easily cleaned, well-balanced, plastic composition (I would guess it's a kind of nylon), six-wheel cart that is comfortable and convenient. If you're going to get a creeper, take my word for it: no matter how silly it feels, put it on the floor of the store, get on and off it a couple times, step on the edge to see if it has a tendency to snap at you like a Doberman, and roll around on it a little (not under a saleslady, or she might snap at you like...well, like a valve spring).

It's not as if even the very best of the creepers are without their dangers. We have to rely on a certain amount of common sense from the creeper operator, after all. A couple days ago, while working on ol' Woodpecker, I was lying under the engine, trying to break loose the stuck piston that has occupied my days recently. I was about to raise up to look at something and I realized I was trapped. I couldn't move my head, I couldn't move the creeper, I couldn't look to either side. Something was holding my head tightly in place like a vise.

I relaxed a moment and tried to gather my wits. I could not for the life of me figure out what was going on. Then I got it: jeez, my hair... Okay, I'm an old, unreformed hippy, it's true. And Linda likes me to wear a ponytail. And I like long hair. And...my hair was caught in the wheels of my creeper! I thought that maybe if I lay there long enough, Linda would eventually come out to check on me and either help me or...or...EEEK! call the local volunteer fire department, made up mostly of my friends and buddies, to rescue me from my jam.

Oh, sure, you bet! That's exactly what I need—four or five of my friends to find me like this. They'd probably call in the local newspapers to take photos before extracting me from my fix. I can see the headlines now: "DANNEBROG VOLUNTEER FIREMEN RESCUE LOCAL DOOFUS FROM DUMB FIX!" And knowing them, they'd strap me to a rescue board and carry me out, creeper and all. And then shave my head to get me loose. With those thoughts of horror, I decided I would get free of that creeper if I had to tear the hair right off my scalp or dismantle the creeper behind my head, working with a set of mirrors.

Actually, my escape wasn't that dramatic. I finally managed to push against the tractor above me and get out from under the tractor and my hair rolled out from under the creeper, but if ever there was a moral to a story, while there is always some risk in any shop, a nick or scrape here or there is nothing compared to humiliation in front of all your buddies up at the tavern.

There are also tool creepers, little trays on wheels into which you can put your tools and parts. Some of them are magnetic so your tools and parts won't fall off. I have a couple of these but I usually wind up forgetting them and using a cottage cheese box instead. Works fine.

Now we're getting down to the doodads and frills in the way of shop tools. I have a couple engine stands, one I use for engines and the other for transmissions, but I know I'm going to be working on a lot of tractors and engines in my life. With an engine stand I can move the engine around the shop easily and safely, turn it over, clean it, re-assemble it, whatever I want with maximum ease. If you're only going to restore one or two engines...? Not worth the trouble, I suspect. Just set your engine on some blocks, being sure it is good and stable. Those engines are heavy rascals. Nobody really needs two stands; the second one is just a convenience for me.

With a Little Help From Your Friends...

My buddy "Bondo" Adams dropped by one day when I was working like a dog trying to sharpen the huge blades on a shredder I use to cut the large stands of native grasses around our house—it's like tinder in the late summer and early autumn. I was filing away, and bleeding, and cussing, and Bondo said, "You know, why don't you just buy yourself a ninety-degree four-inch grinding tool for that job? You're going to have to go through this same mess again next fall and with a grinder, you could do the job in a matter of minutes, and you could use it to grind off that messy weld on the block of Silent Orville."

Well, I'm stingy with my money when it comes to tools that I need for practical jobs around the farm and house and this grinder thing sounded pretty practical, but Bondo really rang a bell when he added that this is something I might be able to use on my Allises! So I got one, and boy, have I used it! I bought a good grinder (Makita) for a surprisingly modest price—less than $50 as I recall—and while I don't use it every day in the shop, it is rare that a month goes by when I don't need it, and need it bad.

I managed to convince Linda that we needed a power washer around the farm to blow dirt off our vehicles. I didn't mention tractors.

The very first job in any restoration or repair job is cleaning the years of dirt off the object of your affections. Eventually this will come down to scrubbing pads, wire brushes, putty knives, even dental tools, but it sure is nice to get a jump on the job by having a power washer available. A power washer takes water from your regular faucet and gives it a lot more force by passing it through a high pressure pump. Most power washers can automatically add soap to the water as you use the machine and the really good (and really expensive) ones heat the water up before it blasts out the end of the nozzle. Great idea but too pricey for me.

My power washer is a fairly small machine, adds soap but does not heat the water. It is good for washing the cars and pickup truck and can blast the worst of the dirt off an old tractor and save me the trouble of scraping it off in the shop and sweeping it out the door later on. Frankly, if we didn't use it for other farm and household jobs, the power washer wouldn't be worth the money. The one car wash in town won't let us wash anything but automobiles with their equipment (and, boy, can I understand that!) but it's not hard or expensive to find a good power washer at a rental shop, especially one that rents tools and construction equipment. You have to wash a lot of tractors to make a purchase worthwhile.

At this point you are probably feeling a little queasy about all the money we're talking about spending. The thing is, you don't buy all this stuff at once. First you have to sense that you need a tool. Then you should read up on it in catalogs and tech manuals and find out what your options are. Then you have to convince yourself that the money would be well spent. And then you have to convince the Little Lady.

In my case, Lovely Linda has never denied me a tool because she knows how much agony I have gone through in my own mind before I bring the issue to her. She always says it's none of her business, that I work hard enough and enjoy my tractors enough that I should have what I need, and that she trusts my judgment. And it's true: whatever doubts there are about spending the money are my doubts. So, I buy a new welding helmet. And then she goes out and buys a new couch.

And of course the joys of good tools are my joys. I really do think there is something going on between men and tools and their shop. Jim Harrison, poet and screenwriter, was once sitting in our front room, enjoying some good single-malt Scotch, and we got to sharing our innermost fantasies. Jim was the food columnist for Esquire, so he knows food, and I am widely known as a serious and dedicated eater, so we talked about food. And we're men, so we talked about tools. And we talked about tractors. And we talked about women. You know how it goes. Anyway, we decided that what we would do the next day is go on up to town and buy the service station that was for sale. Our plan was to convert the wing currently used for repairing tires into a tool store, carrying nothing but the very best tools. We'd put a couple old tractors in there, right with the tools, so if you wanted to test the heft of a three-quarter-inch drive breaker bar with an inch-and-a-quarter socket on a frame-bar bolt, you could do it right then and there. It would be a little like a tool chapel.

And in the other wing, currently wasted on auto repair and servicing, we'd have a fancy restaurant. We'd put a couple tables where nothing but gourmet meals would be served. You'd have no choice, no menu, no decisions. A perfect meal would be planned and prepared a couple evenings a week, and that's what you'd get—perfect salad, perfect bread, perfect wine, perfect entree, perfect side dishes, perfect desert, perfect cheeses, perfect coffee, perfect after-dinner drinks. Between courses you could wander over to the tool section to jostle down the last course and get ready for the next.

The food, we decided, would be served by beautiful, completely naked ladies (our theory is that most health problems in restaurants come from all those spaces and pores in cloth) and would be presented on the best china, crystal, and silver.

We paused a moment to ponder our genius and Jim, for some reason jarred back into reality, blew everything apart, remarking, "You know, Rog, sure as we put together a beautiful package like this, someone will tell us there's a stupid rule somewhere requiring us to open the place to the public!" I'll bet he's right.

Well, I'll never have the Perfect Restaurant, but I can pick up a few of those tools.

I agonized for months and months whether I should buy a welder and/or a compressor. Those are fairly big-ticket items, after all, and if you saw our monthly tool and parts bills...well... I talked with my mechanic friends and they weren't much help. They couldn't imagine me calling my room a "shop" as long as I didn't have a welder and a compressor. My dilemma was that I wasn't entirely sure how useful a compressor would be (I had been dismantling tractors and working along quite nicely on restoration for several years without a compressor, so...?) and while I knew I needed to get some welding done, and I would eventually have to learn how to weld, and probably could learn how to weld, it seemed kind of dumb to buy a welder before I knew how to use the blasted thing.

So I bit the bullet and bought the compressor—a modest, three-horse model on wheels. I picked up a simple set of attachments—tire chuck, air gun, and an impact wrench with a small set of sockets, which seemed to me to be something that would be useful taking off stuck nuts, wheel lugs, etc. And boy, was it. The first time I put that thing to work while dismantling a tractor for parts, I was dazzled by the ease with which rusty nuts were turned off, nuts I would have normally sweated over for hours. Okay, I said I'm in no hurry in my tractor work, but I'm also fifty-eight years old; okay, I'm still in pretty good shape, but I'm no spring rooster any more either. That compressor and impact wrench has made me a much happier fellow.

Since then I have picked up a couple more very cheap air tools (air tools run a lot less than their electric counterparts)—a drill, cut-off tool (for light metal cutting), grease gun, and nonimpact wrench. I still use the air mostly for cleaning out parts (for which it is terrific) but my conscience is now clear about the purchase. I suppose I will eventually pick up a sand blaster and spray paint outfit but for the moment they are not in the picture. What I will probably do with the first tractor I actually restore (rather than simply repair) is haul it to my friend Bondo's shop and work with him on fixing the sheet metal, cleaning, and painting it. Bondo is generous with his information—a lot more about this aspect of restoration later—and while it'll cost me more for him to do the job than for me to do it myself, I'll consider the expense "tuition" and come home with a lot more than a nicely painted, dent-free tractor. I'll come home with an education.

The only thing I've ever sneaked into the shop without Linda knowing is my shop press. It wasn't all that expensive—a touch more than $100—but I probably could have gotten along without it, driving seals and bearings in place with a light hammer or taking them into town and having machinist Don Hochstetler or service station owner Al Schmitt press them in for me with their big presses. Maybe that's why I had the UPS man deliver the package directly to the shop door and then get out of the farmyard as fast as possible: I knew I ordered the press simply because I wanted it, not because I needed it. Well, now I have it and I use it. And now Linda knows I have it. ("Honey, sweetpie, punkin'-darlin', that press is just the thing to put new brushes on your vacuum sweeper, no kidding. It's the one tool I have that will work on something other than a tractor. Are you ever going to be happy we have that twelve-ton brute out here in the shop. In the long run, you're going to be one grateful wife, yessirree, believe you me.")

And a little more than a year after I installed the compressor, I bought an electric welder. It was a Christmas present. From me. What I did was save everyone the trouble of trying to figure out what to get me, and then to sort out what kind of welder I would most want, and...well, being the nice guy I am, I saved a lot of people a lot of worry. As I write this, in the winter of 1994–5, I am spending time practicing running beads and making welded joints, cutting holes and brazing, experimenting with different sizes and grades of welding rod, fooling around with a carbon-arc torch, and having a lot of fun doing it. Okay, I've started a few little fires around the shop, and put some holes in overalls, and divots in my skin, and wasted a lot of welding rod and scrap iron (every couple weeks I go to a local welding shop and dig through the scrap bin for practice materials), but I am learning something new. And Dad always said I should have a trade. (Seriously, for me that's what this is all about—learning new things. I read some place you can't get old while you're learning. The way things are going with this tractor work, I should live forever!) And for Christmas, lovely Linda bought me a shop vacuum cleaner. God, I love that woman.

Chapter Four

Safety Equipment ◆

*I*can't imagine why, but here, just as I finished that paragraph on welding, it occurs to me that maybe it's time to discuss safety equipment, perhaps the most important elements of shop equipment. Mechanical work, especially restoration, is dangerous. There are sharp edges, heavy tools and objects, clumsy lumps, sharp points, whirring, catching, tearing wheels, rods, and shafts, crushing jacks and clamps, hot metal, dangerous acids, caustic chemicals, explosive fuels, lung-searing fumes, lung-clogging dust, things that break, shatter, explode, burn, fall, and snare. I am comfortable in my shop, but I try never to get too comfortable, not so comfortable that I forget that list of horrors. This shop is a warm, pleasant, happy place for me; it is also dangerous. I can't forget that, or my shop days may be over.

I try not to hurry with any process to the point where I forget to be careful. I like a good beer, and while I will drink a beer now and then at my workbench, or a schnapps at the end of the workday, I don't consider the shop a place to lose focus on the task at hand. Don't drink and drive; don't drink and drill, either. I try to stay alert. If I am concentrating on cleaning a carburetor or banging loose a stuck piston, I try to remember to stand up now and then, look

around, check on all the other things going on the shop—the fire in the stove, the parts in the solvent tank, the exhaust fan. Just in case.

As I try to do with everything in my life, I laugh off the times I haven't been careful enough. A couple years ago I pulled my International 300 farm tractor (the working tractor of our stable of machines) into the shop. Water had gradually gotten into the oil of the hydraulics system and things were freezing up. We need that tractor to bring in firewood, clear snow from the drive, get to the smokehouse...we can't get along out here without that tractor and its hydraulic system.

I drained as much of the contaminated oil as I could and then decided that what I probably needed to do next was start the tractor, warm up the hydraulics to break loose ice crystals and move more fluid back to the reservoir where I could drain it. It was extremely cold outside so I didn't want to open the doors or windows. I'm not stupid, so I know that carbon monoxide is lethal, but I'm also not as sophisticated as I should be about such things and, no kidding, I thought it took that dreadful killer-gas an hour or two to work its damage. Since I was only going to run the engine a few minutes, there wouldn't be any problem, right?

Wrong. I started the engine and went to work on the hydraulics. I probably got caught up in what I was doing and worked a little longer than I thought I would with that engine running   maybe ten or fifteen minutes at the most. And all at once I felt myself going down. The interior of the shop took on a funny color and light and I realized just in time, thank God, how stupid I'd been. I made it to the door and got outside into the bitter cold air. I sucked as much of it in as I could. I was sick and queasy, but I think it was more from the realization of how dumb I'd been than from the effects of the carbon monoxide.

I opened all the shop doors, went back in to turn off the tractor engine and headed for the house. I told Linda what I had done and that maybe she should keep an eye on me. She wanted to call the doctor but I insisted that I was okay, just a little sick, and after a rest I'd be fine. And, again thank god, I was. (I didn't know it at the time but of course Linda did call the doctor; he said that as long as I was up and cogent I was probably okay. But, he said, "Keep an eye on him and if he starts to act goofy this evening, better give me another call." Linda asked, still worried, "Regular goofy or peculiar goofy? Rog gets goofy every evening.")

I suspect I really wasn't all that goofy that evening. I think I was considerably sobered by a mistake that could so easily have been fatal. I don't care how cold it is, I don't run an engine—even a lawn mower engine—in that shop anymore without having all doors open. (In fact, now that I think of it, I don't think I have run an engine in that shop under any conditions since that day.) My daughter Joyce didn't have much money to spend that Christmas but she blew over $50 on a good, electric, audio alarm carbon monoxide detector, which I keep installed at all times and test with enthusiastic regularity. As you can guess, I strongly recommend that you have a top-of-line carbon monoxide detector (not one of those little cards on which the card turns color when carbon monoxide is detected—a lot

The Flat Tire Trick

From The Nebraska Farmer, *"The Liar's Corner," November 1994*

In the last column I told you about my pathetic cousin, Jim Glenn, out in Ogallala. He claims I got him interested in old tractors, and now his wife Dorothy won't talk with him (Jim, a lot of guys would pay me to teach them *that* trick!), and he expects me to smooth things over. Okay, I'll do it this once, but I hope everybody doesn't expect me to sort out their marital problems just because I know so much about tractors.

Jim writes, "Roger, Roger, Roger—How do you manage to stay married and love old tractors *at the same time*? Dorothy isn't even speaking to me any more. I wonder if you have the same problem with your Allises that we have with our Case and Oliver: the tires are always flat. And we have discovered that one of the first questions you need to ask when picking up an old tractor is 'Does the steering work?'

"We took your advice and tried to convince our wives that the tractors are actually not junk at all but fashionable lawn decorations. And we now have two lawn decorations, having added an Oliver to the Case. (For the fair we are leaving the Case in its original color—rust!)"

Well, Jim, I hardly know where to start. "Does the steering work?" is not the first question you need to ask if the tractors you buy are like the last two I picked up. They don't have steering wheels. No doubt in my mind: steering doesn't work.

If you're smart, you will leave all of your tractor tires flat. A month ago Linda came home from Grand Island and I asked, "Notice anything new?"

"Not another tractor, I hope," she said.

"Yep, it's orange and has flat tires."

"Roger," Lovely Linda sighed, "*All* your tractors are orange and have flat tires."

The point is, Jim, she didn't even notice I had added another WC to my inventory. And *that, Jim, is our ultimate goal! Believe me, when they lose count, we're on our way.*

of good it will do you as you pass out to see that little card with a different colored button!).

I keep two fire extinguishers in my shop—a big carbon dioxide tank at the workbench on the work bay side and a large utility, powder-type extinguisher just inside the shop door. I also try to keep water at hand for cleaning and as a possible fire extinguisher if needed.

(You probably know this already, but you don't want to put water on an oil, kerosene, or gas fire because it will only spread the fire around. The closest I have come to a fire in my shop was hot welding sparks falling on a piece of wire insulation in a waste bucket. A splash of water put it right out.)

Probably the most important safety device I have is Linda. When I am in the shop, especially if I know I am going to be working with something dangerously heavy, hot, sharp, unsteady, or toxic, I let her know and ask her to check with me a couple times during the morning or afternoon, just in case. Besides, it's nice to see a pretty face now and then, right?

It only makes sense to use the best helmet, glasses, apron, and gloves you can afford when working with something as ferociously hot as welding. When I started welding, I joked with my friend Eric when he asked if I was taking appropriate precautions, "Yeah, I got a good pair of sun glasses that should do just fine."

"Sure," he responded, as soon as he could see I was being silly. "In fact, that arc is so bright, you can just close your eyes and see it through your eyelids!"

Less obvious may be the necessity to wear gloves when working with hot pieces of steel at the bench grinder or a face shield or safety goggles when pounding on a stuck valve, putting a new edge on a chisel, or lying on a creeper breaking loose a rusty radiator bolt. Clear plastic face masks and safety goggles are cheap and relatively comfortable (considering!), even if you wear glasses, as I do. If you don't wear eye protection, sooner or later you're going to wish you had.

Same with your ears. Linda always gives me a bad time about my affection for loud rock and roll music—I was a hippy in the sixties and seventies so I have an obligation to tradition—but it's the scream of a four-inch grinder or the slamming of an impact wrench that worries me. So I keep a pair of sound protectors—those puffy earmuff kind of things—hanging handy at the workbench; they're cheap and they make life a lot more comfortable, not only in the shop but in the house when I want to hear a radio or television over the buzzing in my head!

I'm not a nervous Nelly. In fact, I tend to be pretty skeptical about most safety devices and am just as prone as the next guy to figure it takes too much time to be safe. But I began to find when I was blowing the dust out of engine parts, grinding welds, using a hone to take the glaze off new cylinders, the kinds of things that generate dirty, metallic dust, that my lungs seemed downright congested after an hour or two. On the other hand, once I started snapping on a cheap, disposable mouth-and-nose mask, I didn't have those kinds of troubles. What really convinced me was the first time I looked at the outside of one of those masks after an hour of grinding—utterly filthy with junk that would otherwise

True Tractor Tales

From The Nebraska Farmer, *"The Liar's Corner,"* October 1992

A few months ago I told you how much I love my 1937 Allis Chalmers WC tractor and that I've decided to pick up a few disabled WCs for parts and maybe another "runner" or two, depending on Lovely Linda's patience, and start fooling around seriously with those orange lovelies. And I mentioned how impossible it seems to be to keep those things from running.

Well, I have another example for you: last week I woke up one morning to hear my Allis WC humming away out in the machine shed, which surprised me because no one but me has started that thing for fifteen years. (Unless you count the time I had trouble with sparrows getting into the shed and starting the Allis by landing on its crank. You can bet I was careful not to leave that thing in gear! I solved the problem of sparrows starting the WC by oiling the crank handle so they just slide off if they try to use it for a roost.)

Anyway, I ran out to the shed and there the Allis was, perking along, but not a soul in sight. I thought maybe it was a buddy playing a prank, but the same thing happened the next morning, and the morning after that, too. The next day I got up before sunrise and watched the shed for unauthorized action—but darned if that tractor didn't just start up, and I didn't spot a thing!

Next day I went out and watched that tractor up close. About sunrise a little breeze came up and all at once the tractor crank just turned over and the engine started. Turns out, I had backed that tractor into the shed, so the front end was sticking out. When the usual morning breeze came up, it apparently caught the cooling fan and turned the engine over, starting it up. I turned Sweet Allis around in the shed and haven't had trouble since, so that must indeed have been the problem. Would have been a terrible waste of gas but the Allis hardly uses any.

(Mid-March 1993) Wayne North of Pawnee City writes, "Years ago I had a good gentle-broke John Deere that was an easy starter like your Sweet Allis. It was in July and one of those Kansas thunderstorms came up while I was plowing wheat stubble. Not wanting to get my shoes muddy, I drove that old D right next to the back porch and jumped across. Well, the next evening it was getting towards sunset when I heard that old D start booming. I thought it was the kids but when it didn't stop, I had to shut it off. The kids denied starting it so I decided it was my fun-loving neighbor. So next evening once again it started to boom, but it couldn't be the neighbor as I was watching him slop the hogs. The next morning my wife remarked how much mud had left the hog wallow. Well, I hadn't had hogs for years so decided the neighbor's sow had been over and carried a good load of mud home. About evening I wandered down to the wallow to see about hog tracks. No tracks—but thousands of mud dauber wasps carrying off mud as fast as they could fly. So I followed them and found them flying straight to that old John Deere. When I got there, to my surprise the flywheel started to turn and the old girl started booming. Those mud daubers had been building a nest on the inside of the fly wheel and when it got too heavy, it was off balance and set to turning. Well, that big bore and loud boom pulverized the mud nest and it dropped on the ground. By this time the old girl was about high centered on discarded dauber nests, so as long as it was running, I drove it off to where it was safe from daubers. For years people who came to our place wanted to know why I had a badger mound at the back door. I told them it was no badger mound but a mud dauber's nest. You know, I don't think they believed me."

Wayne, lots of times I make fun of people who write to this column swearing that they are telling the truth, but this time I know you're being square with me. And dear readers, no kidding, this *is* the truth. Last night, as fate would have it, I was working under my AC/WC and found a mud dauber's nest on the flywheel. I was thinking that was a pretty good indication of how smooth that thing runs, but then I got to wondering about how the heck they got in there, since the flywheel is back between the clutch and the block rather than outside, like Wayne's tractor's.

As far as I can tell, that Allis engine runs so cool and easy, that the wasps had flown into the breather, down into the oil pan and back through a little teeny break in the back oil pan seal last fall when I was using the Allis to drive my buzz saw down by the woods. (January 1994) I was sitting on an Allis WC, waiting for the big parade in Stromsburg to get started last June, when someone strolled up— I didn't get his name—and remarked that those WCs were pretty good machines. I allowed as how they still are, and he said that he could recall when he was a boy, his dad got into an argument one morning with two of his neighbors who were accumulating some coffee at the local gossip shop. The first said, "Yep, I plowed five acres this morning with my Minneapolis Moline and it only used a gallon of fuel."

"That's nothing," said the second. "I plowed five acres this morning with my John Deere, and it only burned a cup and a half of fuel."

My Stromsburg friend's father thought a moment and said, "That's pretty good, but today I plowed ten acres with my Allis WC and all I had to do was dip a cob in some waste kerosene and wire it up top the air intake!"

have gone up my nose, down my mouth, and into my lungs. I think I have time to put on the dust mask!

One of the first things I bought when I put my shop together was a top-notch, complete first aid kit in a large metal box. And an extra box of large Band-aids. So far, knock on wood, in my four years of shop work, I haven't had to resort to that box (but I have used plenty of the Band-aids). Which is not to say I haven't hurt myself. An old friend, Russ Meints, a professor at the University of Oregon at Corvallis, says he has a four-knuckle rule when he works in the shop; whenever he reaches the point where he has bloodied four knuckles, he calls it a day. I'd put in short days if I followed that theory. I come in every day I spend in the shop with a couple cuts, a few nicks, a bruise or two, a little burn here, a scuff there, scratches, divots, blisters, splinters (metal and wood), blackened finger nails, maybe even a limp, but nothing serious so far. I'm still glad to have that first aid kit ready when I do need it, and the time will surely come when I will.

I almost hate to admit this one: I drove one of my WCs up to town on a particularly nice day and went into the tavern to have a couple beers with my buddies—strictly to gather information for another tractor job I was working on, I assure you. Well, supper time came around and I grabbed that tractor's crank, as innocent as a babe.

One of the first things I learned about cranking a tractor came not ten days after I got Sweet Allis. Mel Grim, then proprietor of the Dannebrog service station, saw me about to start her, and he stepped up quickly and said, "Rog, I started an old Ford like that once and broke my nose, my thumb, and nearly broke my jaw. When you take hold of that crank, keep your thumb on the same side as the rest of your hand." And he showed me. "And don't start down with that crank. Put it at the bottom of its swing and pull up. It's only a half turn but if your tractor is well tuned, that will start it, and you're far less likely to get hurt." And, generally speaking, that's what I've done since then.

Except this time. I put my thumb on the right side, right along the rest of my hand, but I started at the top of the cranking circle. Don Hochstetler told me later that another thing I should listen for is the distinctive "clink" of the "impulse"; if that clink isn't there, tap on the magneto housing a couple times, hopefully to shake it loose, and turn the crank slowly to see if the impulse has broken loose. If that impulse is not loose, you might have the crank slam back and...

And damn near break your arm, just like it did that day. I'm sure the surprise on my face was even more obvious than the pain. I had no idea that crank would come back so fast. And so hard. I looked at my right wrist. Within seconds it had swollen—and I am not exaggerating—to the size of a grapefruit—a huge, red, throbbing grapefruit. I suspected I had broken my arm. But I sure wasn't going back into that tavern and make a general announcement of my stupidity.

I managed to drive back home and get some ice on the arm, and the swelling went down in a couple days, and I was lucky—it wasn't broken. But I was also lucky because I learned something real big without getting hurt permanently. I make my living writing, and if I lost that right arm for even a few weeks because of something stupid like a mule-kick tractor, well...I wasn't going to be happy, and that's for sure. Now I do two things to avoid that problem, besides pulling the crank up, listening for the impulse clink, and keeping my thumb on the same side as my hand: 1) whenever possible, I start my old tractors by pulling them—Antonia has learned to drive her little Allis C and pull my big Allis WCs; and 2) I cut a couple pieces of four-inch PCV plumbing pipe about six inches long and I keep them handy in the shop and the machine shed and I carry one with me whenever I drive a crank tractor. I pull this short, heavy sleeve over my right wrist when I crank.

Yeah, the boys in town gave me a lot of hoo-ha-ing the first time they saw it, but all I have to do is remind myself of what my arm looked like and felt like on the occasion of that kickback, and I go right ahead with my patented Roger-O Anti-Kickback Tractor Crank Sleeve. Laugh if you will, but if your right arm is important to you, you might want to consider making one or two of your own heavy plastic sleeves.

Chapter Five

Supplies

◆

*B*elieve me, if you want an argument, just mention in a country tavern what you think is the best penetrating oil on the market. Or off the market for that matter. WD-40, Liquid Wrench, Mystery Oil, Kroil, numbered stuff, lettered stuff…it's not simply a matter of effectiveness, it's a matter of personal conviction, a matter of religion. And it's not just stuff off the auto shop shelf. When you get a bunch of Old Tractor Boys together, you get personal and secret formulations on top of that—olive oil, transmission fluid, Coca-Cola, kerosene, paint thinner, diesel fuel, even vinegar and Lime-Away. You'd think you were in a chemist's lab rather than a mechanic's shop!

And that's going to be true of a lot of the supplies we'll be talking about. I'm not trying to tell you what to use, or what's best to use, or even what all the choices might be. I'm just letting you know how things have gone with me in these adventures with old iron. Wherever I need a lot of penetrating oil—filling the cylinder of a stuck piston, for example, it becomes a practical problem and I use kerosene or diesel fuel because I can't afford to dump a half gallon of Liquid Wrench or Kroil into a stuck engine where it will probably drain down into the oil pan and be lost for anything but the waste oil barrel anyway.

On the other hand, I have learned not to underestimate the remarkable penetrating, lubricating, dissolving, liberating capabilities of commercial preparations. I don't know how they work but they sure do. (Sue Halsey up in town insists that WD-40 cures not only stuck bolts and shifter forks but cures bunions and earaches too!) In part, I make my decisions about penetrants (and a lot of the other stuff discussed below) by their packaging: I don't like buying something I'm going to use a lot of in little tiny cans, especially little tiny spray cans. I want stuff I can buy in half gallon or gallon tins, please. I keep a squirt can of penetrant on my workbench and if I need to get the stuff up into a tight spot I just give it a couple squirts. Right now, I am really enthusiastic about Kroil. The stuff is amazing!

Same with solvents. I like kerosene because it does a dandy job but is not as volatile (and therefore as explosive) as mineral spirits, which really cut through dirt and grease on old parts. Kerosene also leaves a thin film of rust-inhibiting and lubricating oil on metal. (When I'm using any of this stuff I turn on my shop exhaust fan or open windows for a good cross draft. I once told a welder who is a trifle, uh, slow, that if he was worried about welding that gas tank, he should just sit on it while working so it couldn't get away from him. There's an old pioneer story about a bonehead at a sawmill who died while trying to ride the big mill's flywheel. His widow remarked, "He was a wonderful husband but he sure didn't know much about flywheels!" I wouldn't like to have folks read on my headstone, "He was a good writer but he sure didn't know much about solvents!")

I keep four small oil squirt cans of kerosene, commercial penetrant, motor oil, and mineral spirits on my workbench so I can use a small amount and put it directly where I want it. I clearly label the cans by tying a short length of colored plastic tape to each spout—yellow for penetrant, red for mineral spirits, blue for oil, orange for kerosene. I also keep a small container of household rubbing alcohol; it's about the only thing that will take off some things like Form-A-Gasket. (For the removal of old, stuck gaskets, I prefer plain old household oven cleaner to the commercial—and usually expensive—gasket removers sold in gearhead catalogs and stores.)

Water can do some jobs none of the above will work for, so I keep a container of water around too; during the winter I keep a coffee can of water on the wood

Sticky Problems

From Natural History, *"Science Lite," October 1994*

I collect and repair old tractors—to be exact, Allis Chalmers WC tractors from the late thirties. It's more than an avocation; dismantling and reassembling old Allis-esis my therapy, my retreat, my obsession. At this point I have...well, I have more orange Allises than I would like my wife to know about.

The thing is, parts for old tractors are hard to find, and therefore expensive, so I am always looking for another WC, mostly to disassemble for parts. Every now and then someone lets me know he has an old Allis WC sitting back in the wood-lot and he'll let me have it for parts for a hundred dollars or so.

As you can imagine, any piece of iron that has been sitting back in the trees for a couple decades develops a good case of rust; in fact, most of the tractors I acquire have over the years become a ton and half of solid rust. Pistons are stuck—in contrast to automobiles, which have "engines" that "seize up" or "freeze," trac-tors have "motors" that "stick"), valves are stuck, crankshafts are stuck, transmis-sions are stuck...carburetors, magnetos, steering assemblies, throttles, controls, plugs, pumps, bearings, seals, gears, lugs, screws, bolts, nuts...all stuck. Rare is the day, therefore, that I am not occupied with the process of getting something *un*stuck.

I'm not alone. My conversations with friends in town often focus on exactly the same sort of problems. Farmers, mechanics, plumbers, electricians, bartenders, cooks—all trying to get things unstuck. Concomitantly, I am amazed at the vari-ety of techniques man has devised getting things unstuck.

Tractor restorers and mechanics often have "secret" formulas for unsticking engines—blends of fine-grade olive oil, brake fluid, transmission oil, vinegar, kerosene, even Coca-Cola. I have listened in on endless conversations arguing the merits of one formulation or another. I pretty much stick, so to speak, to com-mercial unstickers like WD-40 or Liquid Wrench, which I would buy in sixty-gallon drums if I could find a source. Anything to get rid of whatever it is that sticks engines. And in addition, of course, some reliable substance to keep them unstuck.

Mine is the quest that drives a good part of modern technology and warfare, and that drove ancient technology and warfare as well—how to keep your own stuff unstuck or to get the other guy's stuff stuck. Tank treads let your army move without getting stuck; tank traps snarl up the enemy's tank treads so they do get stuck. Oil, grease, graphite, bearings, exotic "slick" materials...all developed to keep chariots, catapults, guns, airplanes, and rockets rolling and sliding; the Allied bombing effort against Germany, on the other hand, was concentrated on the ball bearing plants at Rostock to keep the Blitzkrieg from rolling along smoothly and at Ploesti to deny the Axis the oil to lubricate whatever bearings they did get made. Sticking, unsticking, sticking, unsticking. That's the true dialectic of history.

If this sounds like the sort of simplification an outsider to military thinking might come up with out of ignorance, get this—1) I am not exactly a novice at military tactics, having been a staff sergeant in the Nebraska Air National Guard at one time, and 2) military researchers acknowledge my thesis in their own nomen-clature. They call them "Slick 'ems" and "Stick 'ems," further classified as NLWs, or "Non-Lethal Weapons." No kidding. Slick 'ems slow things down by making them too slippery: they render roads, bridges, and railroads so slimy that both motor traffic and foot traffic are stopped dead—it's like trying to move on ice.

A new stick 'em, on the other hand, was recently described in *Newsweek* (February 7, 1994) as "…a sticky foam that slimes…fearsome gunk, it quickly turns to taffy when exposed to air…bad guys would be stuck until sprayed with solvent." The Rand Corporation's Bruce Hoffman described the stuff as "a polymer adhesive that you drop from a plane or spray on a road, and things just stick. If you glue down the Serbs' artillery, what are they going to do, just throw their guns down and walk away? And could they? The problem is, people stick to it too."

Some folks outside of the military are licking their chops at the idea of getting their hands on this technology. For example, police want to stop miscreants dead in their tracks by zapping them with a canister of super stick 'em or greasing the skids into the slammer with a good dose of slimy slick 'em. I love the idea of a bunch of muggers wadded up in a ball of goo for a couple days; just the company should be punishment enough, not to mention the, er, inconvenience of no convenience, if you catch my drift.

Before long, of course, whatever advantage the good guys have will wind up in the arsenal of the crooks. Police would have to carry not only cans of stick 'em to nail crooks caught red-handed but also a can of *unstick 'em* in case the situation deteriorated into a running goo battle and an officer was gooed by hostile or even friendly fire.

As for us civilians, the world could definitely become a less friendly place if this stuff falls into the wrong hands. I would fight to the death to defend my right to bear slick 'em in well-regulated tractor repair but is there really an argument for public, over-the-counter access to slick 'em? And what will the NRA say? "When stick 'em is outlawed, only outlaws will have stick 'em?"

If the terrible potential of all this is not dealt with seriously, and I mean now, the words, "Stick 'em up" may take on a whole new importance.

stove, to put a little moisture in the air and to give me a source of warm water for cleaning parts. And talk about a cheap solvent! Also, don't forget soap. I keep a small container of regular dish washing soap on my workbench and use it more often than you might imagine. I like WD-40 for spraying cleaned parts before I put them away on parts storage shelves to keep them from rusting. So far, it seems to do the job.

Speaking of cans, I have my wife and mother saving almost every container we empty in our two homes. I am constantly using coffee cans to clean parts, drain liquids, and store parts. I like cottage cheese and butter tubs to clean and store small parts and lids from coffee cans to mix substances like JB Weld for which a clean container is needed which then must be discarded.

JB Weld is remarkable stuff. It is heat-, chemical-, alcohol-, gasoline-, cold-, and wear-resistant. It can be used to repair, seal, build up, and smooth all kinds of parts. An air cleaner is vulnerable to rust more than almost any other component on an old tractor. Moisture is sucked up, blown into, and condensed in the cleaner and it settles to the bottom of the oil reservoir that is usually at the bottom of the cleaner where it captures dirt—and more moisture.

And air cleaners are the most neglected component of an old working tractor because the engine or transmission doesn't stop just because the air cleaner hasn't been cleaned in ten years or is rusting out. Do you recall that I had Sweet Allis almost fifteen years before I got interested in tractors? In all that time, I never serviced the air cleaner. (The operator's manual suggests that it be emptied, cleaned, and refilled daily!) When I mentioned this to Dave Ratliff, the guy who gave me Sweet Allis in the first place, he said, "Yep, that's pretty much the maintenance schedule I had her on too!" Which means that instead of twenty-four-hour care, that air cleaner had been tended to more like every twenty-four years.

Water settles to the bottom of the oil bath in the air cleaner and rusts out the bottom of the oil cup, and when the poor guy comes along who wants to restore that old girl, he is dismayed to find that his air cleaner is rusted out...and so is every other air cleaner he can find on tractors out in the local salvage yard. Believe me, I know that story. I've been there.

Then one day I got a bright idea: I took a badly rusted air cleaner base, cleaned it up the best I could, cleaned off loose metal flakes and flaps, and sanded the whole thing down, outside and in. Then I built up the inside of the base with JB Weld, a commercial substance that comes in two tubes that are mixed and then quickly applied. I let the JB Weld set and then mixed and applied some more until all the holes were filled and the bottom was solid—even though it was mostly solid JB Weld. With my four-inch grinder I shaped and smoothed the filler plastic even with the old steel air cleaner body. Painted, it looks pretty darned good. Sure, an expert could detect the repair and some hard-rock restorers insist this sort of goo-job is a blasphemy. But I am a repairer who likes to take a nonfunctioning machine and make it work again rather than return it to a pristine stage, prettier probably than it was the moment it rolled off the assembly line.

Don't get me wrong: I may get there some day. The time may come when I will be rubbing the thirty-seventh layer of lacquer with extra fine talc rubbing compound, but right now, that's not my passion. If it's yours, you probably won't want to use JB Weld.

On my workbench I also keep a couple tubes of various formulations of Form-A-Gasket for sealing water, oil, and fuel unions, and a small tin of general-application grease. A grease gun is a must (I have two, one hanging outside where I can service tractors without bringing them into the shop and one for shop use). A small roll of plumber's teflon tape is very important for making tight unions in oil, water, and gas lines. I use a lot of various types of radiator sealer for closing the inevitable small leaks throughout the cooling system of a newly assembled engine; I haven't found much difference between the most expensive and the cheapest except the cost.

An expensive but crucial leak sealer is gas tank sealant. This is not easy stuff to use. You have to purge the tank very well to begin with—I use soap and hot water and throw a couple lengths of snow chain inside to break loose scale and rust while I slosh the tank around on our parking slab for a half hour—a real pain in the back, literally. Then I rinse and rinse and rinse. I inspect the inside of the tank with a flashlight and often have to start all over again if the interior is not clean.

Sometimes mechanics use an etcher to really clean out a gas tank, and then the sealer is poured in—the whole can—and the tank is rolled around and around until every possible crack and cranny is covered. I once tried to save money by using only a half a can and I wound up having to do the job twice. When you're done, you can put the sealer back in the can and you may have enough for another gas tank or a small tank, but it is important to use the whole can of sealer while you're sealing.

For cleaning parts I have a big box of scouring pad sheets. The pads are really much too large for my use, so I cut them down and use small patches. As a result, a box of these things lasts me for years. I use fine grade emery paper for final, fine cleaning of parts. Again, emery paper comes in such big sheets, I always tear off smaller pieces for use at my bench. It's not cheap stuff but I am stingy enough with it that it lasts a long time.

I keep two kinds of cloth rags—one-use discards I throw away and keepers I launder with my shop aprons. It's not always easy to find shop rags but I insist that no cloth thing leave our house without me getting a shot at it. Last Christmas I told my dad that if he really wanted to get me something special that he would know was a welcome gift, he could go over to the Goodwill store close to their home and buy me a couple pounds of rag stock, which he did. As a result, I have a good-size square, plastic garbage can under my shop bench full of good, clean, soft cloth rags I can use once and throw away. (And please, every day when you finish working in your shop, take that discarded rag bucket and get rid of it. Throw it out or throw it into the woodstove. Those things can combust spontaneously and all those tools and tractors you love may go up in smoke. For the same reason—uneasiness about the potential for fire—I use a metal bucket for my dirty rags.)

I have another, smaller container of reusable cloths I use for cleaning my hands. Terry cloth is wonderful for this, so I beg Linda and Mom to save their old washcloths and towels for me. These cloths I wash and carry back out to the shop for another use. They get to looking pretty grungy toward the end, just before they become discard rags, but they make the end-of-the-day cleanup a lot easier. I have used paper toweling and it is nice, but I find it a bit wasteful and prefer cloth.

Local mechanics tell me that renting shop rags can be a good deal, even for an amateur like me, because the service is relatively inexpensive and you always have a supply of clean, lint-free rags. At this point, I have enough free rags; renting more would be overkill. I am also concerned about having oily rags piled up between trips to the rag rental shop.

I hate to admit how dumb I was when I got started in this mechanicking thing, and God knows, I have plenty yet to learn, but most of my life, on those rare occasions when I got my hands greasy, I used gasoline to clean them, then washed off the gasoline with Lava soap. Gas works, but it is dangerous as a fire hazard and murder on your skin, even if you aren't trying to maintain a satin soft complexion, with the Lava putting a fine finish on the chap.

The first time I tried the commercial hand cleaner called Goop, I couldn't believe the result. My filthy, greasy hands were suddenly—good grief!—CLEAN! I was flabbergasted. Why didn't all those books on tractor repair tell me about this, I wondered. And I swore that if I ever did a tractor book, I sure wasn't going to make that mistake! A couple years ago Mel Grim, who was then proprietor of the town service station, gave me a gallon jug of a pink, liquid hand cleaner he used—MALCO, it's called—and I have been hooked on it every since. Amazing. Mel told me to have Linda rub a little of the pink liquid into any grease spots on my overalls and it would take those out too, but considering the fact that my overalls are 99% grease spot by now and Linda has enough trouble with my laundry, I decided I'd let him tell her that little trick sometime. (In fact—and here's a little hint that may save your life—I launder my own shop clothes, aprons, drop cloths, and rags. They're too far down the hygiene ladder for someone as sweet as Linda to worry about. And that should get me off for not remembering our anniversary again this year.)

One of the most useful supplies I have in the shop is a box of newspapers. I put them under a leak to keep my floor clean. I have an inch or so of newspapers on my workbench so when one layer gets dirty, oily, or torn, I simply pull it off and toss it in the wood stove. I put dirty parts on a piece of newspaper until I can find time to take it outside to the parts shed. Good stuff.

I have three rolls of wire hanging in my shop—seventeen-, nineteen-, and twenty-two-gauge galvanized wire I use for safety wire (which goes through holes in bolts or nuts to keep them from vibrating loose—rod cap nuts, main bearing cap nuts, brake set nuts, shifter fork set screws, etc.) and cleaning small holes (in a carburetor, for example), and a coarser fourteen-gauge wire for hanging parts.

While wire is useful—probably its principal use—to clean out fine holes and ports in the carburetor, magneto, transmission, oil lines and holes, I also always keep an envelope of pipe cleaners on hand for the same purpose.

Finally, while I have been able to buy ready-made gasket for most purposes (I'll talk with you about this more when we get to the chapter on resources), I also have rolls of a variety of gasket stock, everything from thin papery material through various thicknesses of cork to heavy asbestos stock, so I can make my own gaskets if I need to. Whenever I make a gasket, I try to use either the old gasket or a new one, if I can find one, as a template, a pattern, for cutting the new one. I trace the form first on a stout piece of cardboard and cut out the template with a tool knife. That model template I put in an old cookie box labeled "Gasket Templates" I keep for future reference. Then I cut the new gasket.

I have various other jars, cans, and boxes of stuff I use now and then, more or less, for better or worse, but I don't think I'm going to waste your time or mine cataloging it all. Go to a good automotive store like NAPA and shop the shelves, Heaven only knows what you'll find—stuff you didn't even know existed, I'll bet—nut lock, graphite, carburetor cleaner, tire cleaner, gasket remover, on and on. And you can decide then if it's something you can use or not.

Chapter Six

Resources ◆

*E*ven a master mechanic, veteran farmer, or life-long machinist faces information problems when he tackles the project of repairing, rebuilding, and restoring an antique tractor. A 1938 Graham Bradley is not a 1993 Ford Taurus; a 1916 Case is not a 1993 Deutz-Allis; a 1948 ZTU Minny Mo is not...well, it's not even a 1937 Allis Chalmers WC. The process is peppered with problems: how to remove a mounted cornpicker—I hope I have given you some idea of how much of a problem that can be, where you get replacement parts for a rusted, worn-out one, how the old parts come off and the new ones go on, and what goes in that place where there is no part. If you are a total beginner like me, you don't even know how to loosen stuck parts, how to handle bent iron, dented sheet metal, bent pins, worn gears. Where do you start?

For me, it's more than simply getting things done. I haven't told you the most embarrassing part about the champagne reception I threw for The Giltner when she was rechristened Old Faithful. I was all dressed up in new overalls, just as proud as I could be. Lovely Linda went up to the tavern ahead of me and put up posters and crepe paper. Eric made sure the champagne was

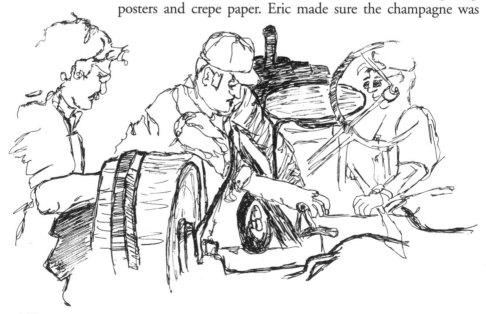

cold and the food was ready to go. And fashionably late, I drove Old Faithful, newly cleaned and waxed, down Main Street to the front of the bar. Everyone came pouring out of the tavern to applaud the resurrected tractor and look her over.

It was a splendid moment. This was my first tractor rebuilding and I was puffed up, but good. I pulled up to the tavern and throttled down as all my friends gathered 'round to admire my machine and my work. I put the tractor in neutral and prepared to dismount so I could join my friends and admire the tractor myself. Whoops. Hmmm. It seemed I was having some trouble slipping the gear shift back into neutral. I pushed the gear shift lever around. Still no neutral. And of course I couldn't get off the blasted tractor as long as it was still running and still in gear. And I didn't want to turn it off because, well, that was the point of bringing her up to town after all.

Talk about embarrassing! Here we were, gathered to celebrate my newly-gained mechanical skills and Old Faithful picked precisely this time to humiliate me. Everyone had his laugh at my discomfort, of course, and then my old machinist friend Don Hochstetler stepped up, pulled a pair of pliers out of his pocket, quickly turned out the six bolts holding the gear shift tower on the transmission and pulled it off. I thought I'd pretty well put this whole shifter mess into order when I rebuilt the tractor, but obviously I hadn't. Don held up the shifter tower so I could see into it.

"See how that shifter end is worn down?" Don asked. I couldn't but I said I could. "See how it pops out of the shifter rod lugs when I move it around?" I couldn't but I said I could. "See how I move that end back into the lug?" I...well, you get the idea.

Don jiggled things around, put the shifter unit back on the transmission and said, "Put her in neutral." I did. This time the lever moved easily and firmly into place. I eased out the clutch. The tractor was content to stay put, even though the engine was still running, and we went into Eric's Tavern to celebrate.

But I didn't forget that dreadful moment. I wanted to know what Don had done. If it didn't take anything more complicated than a pair of pliers to correct, it seemed to me to be something worth learning. So, a couple days later I asked Don if sometime during the winter, when things were slow, he might spend a couple hours with me, explaining just what the hell goes on in that shifter with all those forks, cogs, rods, and gears, and he said he would.

And he did. One cold, winter day he sat me down, took apart the shifter, showed me how things in there worked, and how they go back together. And he took it apart again, saying, "I'll be back in an hour. Have 'er put back together by the time I get back." And I did.

And that's the best advice I have to offer you about where to get information on repairing old tractors. Find those Don Hochstetlers who know what's going on under the lids, hatches, heads, covers, and hoods of tractors, ask them if they will give you an hour or two (I have always made it clear to Don that I understand I owe him money for his time and I am ready to pay, but he hasn't charged me so far) to give you a start at learning that encyclopedia they have tucked away between their ears. Most of these professors are pleased enough that someone finally recognizes and acknowledges their wisdom that they are pleased to take on an eager student.

It takes some backbone, admitting your ignorance, but it's the only way it'll work. Frankly, I think one of my advantages is that I spent most of my life working as a university professor. Imagine what it means to these unappreciated fellows to be able to say that, yep, they taught that smarty-pants professor guy a few things he didn't know.

Ask Mr. Rustoration Answer Man
From Successful Farming, *September 1994*

This is the fourth of my articles appearing in *Successful Farming's* "Ageless Iron" series and so, as you can imagine, I have received a lot of questions from readers about collecting and restoring old tractors. Okay, most of the questions—and the toughest ones, I'll have to admit—have come from my wife Lovely Linda, but I have also gotten a few from other collectors and restorers. (With, I might note, a lot nicer language than Linda uses these days when I drag home yet another battered Allis.)

As Mrs. Gronie, your high school English teacher, used to tell you, "If you have a question, go ahead and ask it because you can be sure that there are other of your friends and classmates who have the same question." In the spirit of Mrs. Gronie's presumption of universal bewilderment, I am going to share some of our readers' questions and my responses with you.

Dear Mr. Rustoration Answer Man,

I'm a beginner, so there are a lot of things I still don't know about this wonderful hobby of restoring old tractors. For example, after a day in the shop, my hands are black with dirt and grease, and I have not found a way to get the stuff off. Days later, even after my knuckles have healed, my fingernails are still ringed with the black grunge.

Drecky in Denver

Dear Drecky,

I'm not sure I understand your problem. I haven't had this sort of trouble since I started stirring my coffee with my fingers.

Dear Mr. Rustoration Answer Man,

Yesterday I was working on a carburetor and dropped a tiny little brass screw. I heard it hit the floor and roll, so I had a rough idea what direction it took, but I could not for the life of me find the blasted thing. It is impossible to buy a replacement. *I must find that screw.* Can you help me, Mr. Answer Man?

Frustrated in Philadelphia

Dear Frustrated,

You bet I can help you. The first thing experienced mechanics do in a situation like this is to try to think like the lost part: where would you go if you were an unappreciated brass screw from a carburetor and you wanted to make the most of this, your moment in the spotlight? That is to say, the experienced mechanic assumes the worst: he immediately goes to the most remote corner of the shop, back behind a pile of filthy, rusted manifolds with razor-sharp edges and filled with mouse nests. Two hours later, covered with dirt, grease, and blood, he reaches the distant, dark corner behind the manifolds and finds…nothing.

The lost screw has out-maneuvered the mechanic yet again. The thing is, that little brass screw knows you are going to look first in the most unlikely place—i.e.—the most likely place. The brass screw will, therefore, be in neither. And that's the heart of the matter: the lost part will never be where you look for it *first*. Ask anyone. Review your own experience. The lost part will always be in the *last* place you look. (But you can't start at the last place, because then it becomes the first place.)

What you have to do is to go ahead and perform your search, even though you now know it won't do you any good. You *must* look in the remote, dirty corner under the manifolds, even though the part isn't there, because…well, just because. In fact, you'll have to look everywhere in the shop, under everything, behind everything, not finding the part, until you're finally so frustrated, you throw a wrench through the window, stomp out of the shop, track grease across your wife's freshly mopped kitchen floor, and mix yourself a stiff drink.

Later that evening you'll find your lost part in the bib pocket of your overalls.

Dear Mr. Rustoration Answer Man,
I have a pretty good mechanical sense but I can't figure out electrical devices like magnetos. How does a magneto work, Mr. Rustoration Answer Man?
Curious in Columbus

Dear Curious,
Magic.

Dear Mr. Rustoration Answer Man,
I put together a real nice shop for working on Old Iron and I have spent many pleasurable hours out there. The problem is, my friends keep borrowing my tools. So, the next time I need a half-inch drive socket ratchet, it's off somewhere halfway across the county. What's to do, Mr. Answer Man?
Looted in St. Louis

Dear Looted,
This is an easy one: get yourself a new set of tools. Then get yourself a new set of friends.

The problem is a lot tougher, of course, when the borrower is your own kid. My pal Slick and I were discussing this dilemma not a week ago. His son had dropped by and helped himself to a car-trunk full of tools just about the same time my kid pulled the same stunt. Slick is a real philosopher, and I think he hit the bull's eye when he shook his head and lamented, "You know, Rog, it's a real shame when our own boys come rolling into our shops and help themselves to our tools, whisking away in a matter of minutes what it took *us* years—YEARS!—to filch from *our* fathers."

continued on next page

"Shame" isn't strong enough a word for it, Slick.

Mr. Rustoration Answer Man,
I am trying to remove a pinion gear from the steering pedestal of my tractor. I was darn near smug about the problem because my wife gave me a three-arm gear puller for Christmas, so for once I was ready with the right tool for exactly this situation. I read the directions for the puller carefully and set about installing the puller on the gear. Hours later I was still trying to wrestle the puller arms in place, get the puller shaft centered, tighten the puller nut, and apply pressure on the gear, all at the same time. Mr. Answer Man, it seems obvious to me after struggling with this thing for the better part of a day that the only way I'll ever be able to use a three-arm gear puller is if I grow another hand.
Baffled in Buffalo

Dear Baffled,
Yes.

Dear Mr. Rustoration Answer Man,
I cannot for the life of me figure out the size of the set-bolts that hold the shifter forks on the transmission shafts of my 1937 Allis Chalmers WC. The square head of the bolt is ever-so slightly too big for a 9/64" wrench, ever-so slightly too little for a 5/32" (10/64") wrench. I took the shifter to a top-notch, fully equipped machinist and he said that he can't figure it out either. He can't even make a 19/128-inch wrench, precisely between 9/64s and 10/64s, fit the bolt head. So what's the deal?
Misfit in Minneapolis

Dear Misfit,
I'm glad you asked this question because I am one of the few guys around who can answer it. Bohumil Brzd, Allis design engineer from 1925 until 1942, chose this charming way to pay homage to his beloved homeland, the Republic of Irregula (absorbed by Metricia shortly after the First World War). The size of the bolt head is, as you correctly note, nonexistent in the modern world. It persists, however, as the Irregulian Pft, based on half the width of a gnat's gluteus maximus. Your only option is to go at that set-bolt with an eighteen-inch pipe wrench. (I know there's no room in the shifter housing for an eighteen-inch pipe wrench, but then that wasn't your question, now, was it, Mr. Misfit?)

Dear Mr. Rustoration Answer Man,
I have been working on old tractors for about five years. I've read everything you write about the subject and follow your advice as closely as I can, so I trust your judgment. Lately I have noticed that my coffee tastes like Liquid Wrench. What's going on?
Yucky in Yuma

Dear Yucky,
Beats me.

Well, there you have it—a wealth of information garnered from many long years of experience. Now all I have to do is come up with some answers for Lovely Linda.

This is really going to sound cold. I don't know how to make it sound right. I haven't gone out of my way, no kidding, to round up friends I can leech information off of. I knew most of these guys long before I became interested in tractors. And some of them trickled along later, like Al Schmitt who took over Mel's service station up in town when Mel decided to retire. It's pretty hard to live in a town of 320 and not know the guy who runs the service station. And how can you be interested in working on tractors in a town of 320 and have the guy who runs the service station not know what you're up to? So, no kidding, I really didn't try to make friends on the basis of how they can help me with my tractor problems, and of course I wouldn't recommend for a moment that you do that either.

But those tractor-wise friends will come along, you just wait and see.

In my catalog of tractor buddies, there's Don Hochstetler, mentioned several times above. He's a master machinist and a general handyman. I've paid him to do some big jobs for me—rebuild a head, weld broken parts, drill stuck lugs out of a manifold, but most of the time I just run into him in the town tavern and he asks what I've been doing (he can tell by looking at me after a day in the shop that I sure haven't been baking an angel food cake!), and I tell him I'm wrestling with needle bearings, and he asks how I'm going at it, and I tell him, and he tells me what he would do in that situation (that is, he tells me what anyone who knew what they were doing would do, as opposed to what a doofus would do), and I buy him a beer, and run home with my head stuffed full of new information. He's not being fooled; he knows what's going on. And he enjoys seeing me get these old girls running as much as anyone because he loves old tractors too.

Sometimes I'm real lucky and a couple other mechanics are in the tavern at the same time, and they join in on the conversation and say how they would do it, and then Don says why that's dumb, and the other guys say why Don's idea is dumb, and Eric gets mad because I'm using up so many bar napkins taking notes on how to deal with needle bearings.

On a couple occasions Don has offered to lend me tools, but I never take advantage of his offer. I don't believe in borrowing tools. I do ask him to show me the tool and how it's used, and then I decide if it's something I should have for myself. And a few times Don has given me spare tools out of the goodness of his heart. That's fair. I'll do that. But I don't borrow tools.

The advantage of Don is that he has been around tractors all his life. He's a machinist, but more importantly, he's a machinist who knows about tractors, and Allis Chalmers tractors, and Allis Chalmers WC tractors. That makes him a pretty valuable friend, you can imagine. My mechanic friends aren't often triple loaded like that. For example, Kenny Porath and Al Schmitt are real mechanics. They work as mechanics, Kenny at the State Shops, Al in his service station up in town. That means they know a lot about engines, hydraulics, body work, and other mechanical problems. The amount of their knowledge astonishes me. But they don't know specifically about Allis Chalmers WCs, or Allis Chalmers, or tractors. But a lot of what they know applies to tractors, and I can go to them with questions.

Same with Bondo Adams. He's a body man, and an Allis WC doesn't have much bodywork to worry about. And Dan Selden is a plumber, and an Allis has even less in the way of plumbing. But Bondo and Dan are also farm boys. They know a certain amount about vehicles because of their trades, but they know a lot about tractors because of their upbringing. They know how to weld, fix, and bend things, and sometimes they know more than professionals because there are some things professionals wouldn't try even if they were working with their worst enemies' vehicles. Bondo and Dan will try anything.

Sometimes that's what it takes. I won't mention any names but I was once stuck in the boonies with one of my mechanic buddies. We were picking up a trailer, but one of the tires was flat. We had an air bubble but the tire was off the wheel's bead, so we couldn't even start getting air into it. I figured we were out of luck, but not my buddy. "Watch this," he said.

He took a can of ether, the kind you use to start engines on very cold days, and sprayed some inside the tire. "Stand back," he said, and tossed a match into the tire. Pha-WOOOOM! The ether exploded, the tire sprang into place, full of the exploded gasses. "Quick," my friend said, and pushed the air hose from the bubble on the tire's valve. He stood up when he had filled the tire, a broad smile on his face. I stood there, mouth open in astonishment. You don't learn that in mechanics school, I'll bet!

I try not to bother my human resources, these walking encyclopedias of mechanical information, when they are working. Mechanicking, bodywork, and plumbing is their business, and frankly, I think they deserve what they earn at their trade as much, if not more, than a doctor earns at his or hers. A doctor works, at the most, on two models of a single make of machine—male and female models of humans; a good mechanic works on dozens of models of dozens of makes—Fords, Allises, Bugattis, John Deeres, Harleys, on and on, over many years of production models. I would no more interfere with a mechanic working on a paying job than I would drop into an operating room during a triple heart bypass procedure to chat with a doctor about how his golf game is going. And I would no more borrow a professional mechanic's 3/4-inch drive 1 1/16-inch socket than I would ask the doctor if I might borrow his #12 scalpel if he's not using it at the moment.

Moreover, when I do ask these guys to do something for me, I pay them for it. It's their job. They make their living from what they know, and when I hire them to use that knowledge, they deserve to be paid for it. On the other hand, I don't mind asking them what they're going to do, what they're doing, how they do it. I don't mind asking them when I run into them at the tavern or in the post office how I might go about shaking loose a stuck oil fitting, or what they use for head gasket sealer, or what type bar puller they prefer, or how they would go about shimming a worn steering shaft guide. If it's a working day and the answer turns out to be a long one, I ask them if I can buy them a beer or soda after work and talk about it then. It's not as if I'm such a generous and considerate guy, after all.

These friends are valuable resources and I don't for a moment want them to come to think of me as a pain in the butt and start avoiding me!

Another flavor of professional, maybe even professional mechanic, is "farmer." As anyone who knows farmers knows, farmers are experts in several dozen categories. You can't be a farmer and not know something about tractors, and engines, and welding, and electrical systems, and on and on (along with all the stuff they need to know about agriculture proper—botany, animal husbandry, earth science, economics, chemistry, politics, on and on and on). These independent folks may not have bosses and regular hours but don't doubt for a moment that they are busy people and don't have a lot of time to waste on your hobby.

But some farmers have reputations for knowing a lot about tractors or Allises or magnetos or hydraulic systems. And some farmers have reputations for being generous with their knowledge. Again, I am darned cautious about taking up the time of people busy earning their living. If I can, I make an appointment to stop by the farm or to meet them in town and take along a six-pack or some fresh bread. At Christmas, I make a point of taking one of my home-cured, home-smoked hams to these people who've been so generous with their time and information, and they are the first ones invited to any tractor's re-baptism reception.

Again, I must say that these folks are generous, if anything, to a fault. They'll take the time, they'll share what they know, and sometimes they'll come into the yard dragging a tractor they picked up cheap at an auction sale, or an old head they found tucked away in one of the buildings on the farm, or some guy they met at the grain elevator who knows the answer to precisely the question you were asking last week. They seem to adopt your project and its problems as their own project and problems.

And sometimes that's the way it has to go. If nothing else, I've learned patience in this process. If I run into a problem—a bum starter on a later model WC, for example—I don't get excited and run out to buy another starter. I ask around. I talk with farmers at the tavern, I ask Al at the service station, I mention my problem to Kenny Porath. In a couple days, or a couple weeks, the nibbles start. Word comes down the line that there may be a guy over in Kearney who has an old WC he dismantled for the engine but doesn't need the starter. And there's another guy over in St. Paul who used to rebuild tractor starters, but he may have gone blind or died since then, and why don't I bring the starter up sometime and we'll take a look at it, right here on a table in the tavern?

So, I toss the malingering starter into the pickup cab and haul it around with me a couple days until I run into The Boys again at the tavern, and they look it over, but doubt that it can be repaired, and besides, the guy over at St. Paul did die—about twenty-seven years ago, as a matter of fact, and by golly, "I think I do have a starter like that back in the machine shed," and "Why don't I just run out and dig it out right now, and I'll be back in a minute," and pretty soon you have a filthy, but working starter sitting there right in front of you, nestled down among the pork rinds and pretzel sacks, and your pals are already dismantling it and cleaning it up and getting it ready to go..., and the price for all this is, "Jeez, Rog, since I didn't even know I had it, it can't be worth much—why don't you just buy me a beer and we'll call the deal good?"

Don't laugh. That's the way it works. I don't know what the heck you do if you live in the city. Sell your house and move to the country, I guess. Actually, I'll bet there's some small tavern tucked away somewhere, or maybe a retirement home where the old guys sit around on the front porch in the sun and watch the traffic go by, where you could find the same kind help, city or country.

Now I'm going to get technical for a second. Not technical about tractor but technical about English. I want you to understand an important distinction, the one between "old-tractor guys" and "old tractor-guys." "Old-tractor guys" means fellows who are interested in old tractors; "old tractor-guys" means old guys who know about tractors. That fine distinction is important because the age of your mechanic resource is unimportant. Some of the very best resources I know in the line of old tractors are men half my age who know more than any old fart I've ever encountered. They are likely not only to know things you need to know but to have things you need to have. Start looking around for those old-tractor guys.

It won't take much casting about and hint-dropping to find out not only who the old-tractor guys are in your neighborhood, but increasingly in this day of specialization, who the old-Allis Chalmers guy is in your neighborhood, and, if you are really lucky, who the old-Allis WC guy is in your neighborhood. Find that guy and go talk with him. He will be glad to know you're interested. He'll be glad to show you what he has. He'll be glad to ask you if you happen to have a set of styled fenders in good shape you might be willing to trade for that radiator you need—and of which he happens to have two.

A great way to find just that sort of fellow is to attend shows, meets, gatherings, fairs, and festivals where old tractors are exhibited. So, how do you know when and where they are going to happen? Well, if you belong to an organization for your kind of tractor, you will find a constant calendar of gatherings. And you can watch your state newspapers. In Nebraska, there is an annual calendar of all the festivals and fairs in the state, published by our state travel and tourism office; it lists dozens of tractor shows and exhibits. But your best bet, all across the nation, is The Annual Steam and Gas Show Directory, published for a very modest price by Stemgas Publishing Company, PO Box 328, Lancaster PA 17603.

I've been surprised here, I'll have to admit. I saw other Allis people around here as potential problems, almost certain to bid against me at the next farm auction where I found an old WC I wanted. And I have had that happen. But I have not yet found someone I couldn't talk with about the situation. If they have their heart set on that tractor, well, I don't bid the price up, knowing I'm not going to get it. If they want it more than I do, then they'll probably get it.

But that's rarely—very rarely—the way it has gone for me. More likely, they'll call and let me know there's a WC coming up at a sale where they are going to bid on a G. And would I like to have them try to pick up the WC for me if it is going cheap? Or I go to a sale and buy a WC and darned if it isn't the other Allis guy who offers to haul the thing home for me. Curiously, there seems to be more room for good feelings and friendship in this old tractor business than for competition and meanness.

Now I'm getting off the topic, but this seems a good place to tell you about another thing I've learned in my short time as an ag-gearhead. From high school on I have avoided gearheads. They are dirty, crude, and arrogant, smell bad, and are impatient with those of us who know nothing about cars and engines. Well, now that I am dirty, smell bad, am crude, and arrogant and impatient with those who know nothing about old tractors, I find that gearheads are actually pretty nice guys. They haven't invested a lot of energy in their social skills, they tend to be a little on the shy side with people who are clearly not gearheads, but aside from my Native American friends, I have not met a kinder, nicer, more generous bunch than mechanics, auto repairmen, parts store people, service station grease monkeys, all those kind. They may be stand offish at first—probably because they've been snubbed by the fancy folks (like professors) for so long—but man, once they know you're willing to get a little grease under your fingernails and know a lug nut from a rod cap—OR THAT YOU ARE WILLING TO ADMIT YOU DON'T AND RESPECT THOSE WHO DO—you won't find a nicer lot.

There. I said it and I'm glad.

Now, are you ready for the next giant step? Say you're a young banker working on a Case VAC, and you're a beginner, and you don't know much about any mechanics, yet any tractor, yet a Case, yet a VAC. And you've nosed around but haven't found a Case VAC mentor yet. And you need an oil pump. And you haven't found a parts tractor, and even if you did, your wife is not about to let you haul in another tractor to sit around for parts. Now what?

My friend, if you are going to work on an old tractor, one of the very first things you should do is find out if there is a club, magazine, society, or organization dedicated to your model or make of tractor. Or dedicated to tractors with the peculiarities of yours. Or old pulling tractors. Or old steam tractors. Or simply old tractors. Join that club immediately. Ask for a list of back copies. See if there isn't an issue that deals precisely with your tractor or the specific problem you are stuck with. These publications are where you'll find out about meetings, conventions, and machinery shows where you'll not only find birds of a feather but spare parts, books, information, and sympathy. And you won't be alone: while you are crawling under that Minny Mo, taking notes on how the exhaust system is supposed to be put together, all around you you will see other enthusiasts, scrutinizing whatever machines they have been trying to figure out, getting the information and ideas they need too. You'll never find a better place to get so much reliable information in such a short time.

Some such organizations—*The Old Allis News*, for example, in my case, or *The Allis Connection*—give you one free classified ad with each year's subscription, and that is a gift from heaven. I am going to deal with publications in an appendix at the end of this book, but for the moment, let me turn the story back to poor ol' Woodpecker again. It became clear to me early on that what I desperately needed for that piece of wreckage was an operator's manual for that model cornpicker. So, where do you go to find an operator's manual for a fifty-year-old piece of farm equipment?

I'd been hoarding my free ad in *The Old Allis News*, waiting for just this moment. I dropped a plea for help to Nan Jones, editor of *OAN*, and she squeezed my cry for assistance into the next issue of the magazine. Within a couple days, a fellow sent me a Xerox copy of exactly what I needed. Several more came later in the week, some offering to sell me the papers (and heaven knows, they would have been worth it to me), some offering to send me copies free. One woman just sent me an original copy and said, "Keep it. It's yours." I can't recall what a subscription to *The Old Allis News* costs but that one ad was worth the whole whatever it is. In fact, I sent Nan a check for the next five years, subscription. I don't want to be caught with my renewal notice down.

Now, to tell the truth, *The Old Allis News* is the second place I went. First, I went to my Deutz-Allis dealer. "Ah, come on, Welsch! You had the nerve to go to a modern farm implement dealer and bother him for information about a fifty-year-old antique?!" Damn right. And he had what I needed. And he let me copy it. And here's the big news: he may very well have the parts for me when I get ready to work on that piece of junk. Since then I've found yet another veteran Allis dealer, and he says he has lots of old parts too.

And that's the next resource you need to nurture—your modern tractor and farm equipment parts dealer. Okay, you probably won't have much luck finding a dealer for a Rumley Oil Pull or Huber, but it doesn't hurt to ask around. In my case, Wayne Hilder and his son Kevin are the Deutz-Allis dealers in Central City, about thirty miles east of my farm. I met them at an auction sale, where they were buying Allis parts, and they quickly spotted what I was buying as Allis parts for WCs. Their business has been in the family forever, and they know Allises up and down. They appreciate, even love, the old machines, just as I do.

New parts, even for old tractors, are not cheap. I recall vividly the day I went to Hilders' with a handful of worn parts—seals, bearings, set screws, that sort of thing—in a two-pound coffee can. I asked if they could find new replacements. They did, and I walked out with a coffee can full of new parts. And $120 less in my pocket. (Before you think I'm complaining, I'll add that a couple days ago I had my Ford Taurus checked for a squeak in the steering wheel and brakes and a nonfunctioning power rearview mirror; simply checking the problems cost me more than $200!)

I think it was when I returned from that trip I showed Linda the can of parts and the bill and said, "Now, the next time you see me hauling another wrecked Allis into the yard, just remember that I paid less for that whole tractor and all its parts than I did for this bucket of new parts." What I didn't tell her, is that when it comes to things like seals, bearings, and gaskets, I'll still be driving over to

Hilders' for new parts.

Frankly, I think the Hilders spend more time with me and my WC problems than they do with someone who comes in to buy a new $100,000 combine. Heaven knows, they have never stinted with their help. Within this past hour Wayne called, working to find some parts for me as cheaply as possible. He gave me information about some parts I thought might fit but will not.

The last time I stopped in the Hilder agency, I mentioned I was working on The Woodpecker and would eventually get to the cornpicker too. "Do you have the cornpicker pulley for the belt drive?" Wayne asked.

"No," I said. "There is a long v-belt wrapped around the regular belt pulley."

"I think we have a couple of the original pulleys that were supposed to be used with those pickers. If you want one, we'll give it to you."

They did indeed have the pulley, and they did indeed give it to me. When your hobby is rebuilding or restoring old tractors, you can't afford not to have friends like that.

I've already mentioned Jim Stromp, salvage yard proprietor extraordinaire. Jim's not only a good friend, and an unpredictable trickster, he runs one remarkable salvage yard. I'll never forget the first time my friend Dan Selden drove me up to Stromp's Dump. I was flabbergasted by what I saw—acres of junked tractors, a full acre of Allises, mostly WCs. Jim's not cheap either, but his used parts cost a lot less than new ones, and often, you'll find things at a salvage yard like Jim's that you simply cannot find anywhere else. In a couple cases, I have bought whole tractors from Jim, so he is not only a source for parts but for whole machines, too.

There's a difference between scrap metal dealers, or junk dealers, and salvage

---

Sacred Ground

From Natural History, *"Science Lite," January 1993*

I changed my mind the moment we came over the hill and I first caught sight of Stromp's Dump. Maybe it was a flash of insight, or maybe I'm just getting older, but what I saw in this junkyard was not the same thing I used to see when I saw a junkyard—rural blight, pollution, ugliness, *junk*.

For one thing, at Stromp's Dump there is a double row of ancient, sheet metal combines flanking the entrance to the place, stretching off to the east and west almost as far as you can see. I'll bet that on the vernal and autumnal equinoxes, if you stand in the right place, maybe over there by that rusting steam traction engine, the sun rises right between that double row of combines, and some day archeologists will write about it.

We drove slowly into Jim Stromp's yard. Jim wasn't home, but we had already been told by several dozen other people who drive hours from all directions to Stromp's for tractor parts that we could go ahead and salvage whatever parts we needed and then just check with him when we left. So we—my daughter Antonia, my pal Woodrow, and I—drove across the yard and through the big iron gate that leads to…The Tractor Yard. *continued on next page*

My 1938 Allis Chalmers WC surprises me a lot—nearly every time I turn the crank, in fact. It starts when it has every reason not to, it pulls better than it should at its age, it runs with almost no care, and uses next to no gas or oil. Then, earlier this year, I got another 1938 Allis Chalmers WC (as I told Linda, you never have too many 1938 Allis Chalmers WCs) and I found myself looking for brake parts.

Where do you get parts for a 1938 Allis Chalmers WC, I wondered? First, Mel up at the Mobil station in town gave me a catalog because, it turns out, you can buy almost any part you need for almost any tractor ever made, including a 1938 Allis Chalmers WC, new or rebuilt, through the mail. I suppose that should have been obvious to me but like a lot of things that should be obvious to me, it wasn't: tractors last forever and so there are a lot of 1938 Allis Chalmers WC tractors still running out there and a lot of them need parts and there are people who take apart tractors that don't run and make those parts available for people like me who need parts.

Mel's revelation opened a new world for me, but it got better—a lot better. Woodrow suggested that we could find parts even cheaper at Stromp's Dump, and have more fun at it. He said we could get things like entire front ends that we'd sure never get through the mail, and from the gleam in his eye, I knew he was telling the truth. So we ran up to Stromp's Dump, a little over an hour away from my farm, and a whole new galaxy opened.

We drove through Stromp's gate and a scene for all the world like Oz or WonderLand stretched before us. I gasped. "Wow, Dad," Antonia sputtered, "there's a green hill and a red hill and an orange hill and..." And she was right, because the hill immediately to our left was covered with hundreds of carcasses of orange Allis Chalmers tractors, the hill directly before us was blanketed with the remnants of green John Deeres. There were red Internationals, and far away, nearly at the horizon, Cases, Olivers, Fergusons, and Whites and...well, all in all, it was an amazing sight: acres and acres of tractors in various stages of wreckage.

Woodrow, who had been to Stromp's before, took a moment to enjoy our amazement and then said, "Let's see your list." I handed him the paper listing the parts I hoped to find—a belt pulley, a front end, two full sets of brake parts, an oil filler cap, that sort of thing—and grabbing his bucket of tools he set off wading through the sea of cannibalized WCs. Antonia and I grabbed our bucket of tools and set off in the opposite direction across Allis Chalmers Ravine.

It was a cold, cloudy day and we worked with some haste, hoping to get our parts and return to the warmth of Woodrow's truck as quickly as possible. As we pulled, twisted, hammered, and pried, other drivers steered their pickup trucks slowly through the yard and stopped near likely sources of parts for whatever tractor they were in hopes of fixing. I heard occasional snippets of conversation over the wind, the sounds of steel tools on steel parts, the unmistakable screech of a crescent wrench burring the corners of a bolt and sliding off, muffled curses, and the sounds of sucking on scraped knuckles.

The Greenies on John Deere Hill spoke of their quests—a wide front end, flywheels, and front steel—and we Orangies at Allis Chalmers Ravine combed through the wreckage for ours—a magneto, a fuel sediment bulb, the bottom half of an air cleaner. Occasionally we looked across neutral ground at each other, grunted a greeting, maybe borrowed a tool, but while it was clear that we were all there for the same purpose (harvesting parts), we were as alien to each other as ancient Pawnee and Lakota miners working within sight of each other at flint quarries.

That was it! That was what changed my understanding of junkyards. I had always thought of places like Stromp's as terrible places, ugly concentrations of litter and ruin, but now for the first time I saw that this was a quarry—a tractor parts quarry. We were all of us—Greenies, Orangies, and Yellowies—engaged in a recycling process, salvaging entire vehicles, piece by piece, scavenging the abandoned to rescue the still serviceable. Like Native Americans at flint quarries, we were sharing a kind of *ad hoc* truce with members of other tribes at work in the same quarry.

Native American Quarriers: "Boy, look at those ugly shagnasties over there hacking away at the worst flint in the quarry; won't those bozos ever learn to make decent weapons? Whatever they're eating smells like it should have been buried a long time ago.

Oh-oh, here comes one of 'em. What? You want to trade some of your elk pemmican for an antler flaker? Yeah, that sounds fair enough. Here, try
continued on next page

a little of this dried chokecherry too. What's that brown flint look like over there? Worth digging?"

Us: "Woodrow, look at that. Those dummies are trying to take off a steering wheel with pliers—as if it made any sense to dink around with John Deeres to begin with. Is he trying to adjust that carburetor with a hammer, or what?! Oh-oh, here comes one of 'em. You want some penetrating oil? Yeah, sure. Here you go. Help yourself. Blackberry brandy? Sounds good. Will it help break those bolts loose? Hmmm, I'll bet. Here, try this socket on that steering wheel. Didn't happen to see the front spindle off'n a square-nose Allis WC over there, did you?"

Different worlds, but for the moment, today, here at Stromp's, we're staying cool and avoiding discussions of religion, politics, and implement lines.

That afternoon, as we drove out of Stromp's with our Allis parts, I wondered if we weren't missing something by leaving so early in the day. I imagined aloud if maybe at night there aren't little campfires scattered around Stromp's Dump, perhaps shadowy figures huddled over them scouring parts with wire brushes, muffled conversations about a nearly virginal sector gear needing only one more pin pounded out before it can be pulled out and taken home. Maybe secret songs are sung, inviting the blessings of gods that protect or vex swathers and combines. On appropriate days are there arcane rituals initiating young apprentices into the secrets of the Massey-Harris clutch assembly, sacrifices to the spirits of internal combustion?

"What do you think?" I asked Antonia and Woodrow.

"Huh?" said Woodrow.

"Let's eat," said Antonia.

---

yard keepers. Jim Stromp buys and keeps machines so guys like me can come to him for parts. (Take your own tools to such places because it will be up to you to remove what you need.) Stan Koperski and Carl Cool here in town are scrap dealers. They go to sales and buy junked farm equipment and old metal for resale; when they get hold of a tractor, as often as not, it's going to be crushed into a little block, sold, and melted down to be recast into Tonka Toys and lawn mower parts.

In a way, that's exactly what I'm looking for—junk tractors, not Tonka Toys or lawn mower parts. I had trouble with one implement-salvage dealer because he kept buying beautifully restored, mint-condition tractors for me. He simply couldn't understand that I don't want beautifully restored, mint-condition tractors, that there's no fun in them for me, that I want junkers I can "part out" or rebuild.

Carl Cool and Stan Koperski know exactly what I want, because it's the sort of thing they look for, too. If they can buy a junk Allis WC, they're just as happy to sell it to me, maybe even happier, than to a scrap metal buyer. Hey, if they buy a tractor for $90 for iron, I don't mind at all paying them $125 for it—the good manifold and magneto alone are worth that—and they get a better deal than they would from a metal buyer. We just have a good ol' time making each other happy!

Finally, maybe my best resource, helper, information source is Lovely Linda herself. I've already mentioned her as a safety device, hauling technician, and nut picker-upper, but she's more than that. And I don't know, but things may be getting better rather than worse. We were driving down the highway not ten miles from here a couple days ago and she suddenly yelled, "Rog, Rog! Over there!!" and she pointed across my bow into a grove of trees. I hit the brakes, thinking there might be a couple deer coming at me, but no, she then said, "Look, right there under that big tree! An old tractor!"

Well, I glanced long enough at the tractor to make sure it wasn't an old Allis, but then I looked back at Linda. From the look on her face, I could see she was as surprised as I was. Linda calling my attention to an old tractor is like Marla Maples Trump saying to The Donald, "Oh honey, look over there! It's a beautiful young woman with a gorgeous figure, and she's smiling at you as if she thinks you are the sexiest thing alive and would do absolutely anything to make you happy!" Phew. That would take the sort of confidence not many folks are likely to have.

I was so proud of Linda, I told her that even if that old tractor had been an Allis, I wouldn't have gone over to look at it or tried to acquire it without her explicit permission and approval. ("Why, yes, Marla. That's my second cousin Heather, and she'll be staying over with us for a few weeks while she gets some housing arranged over at the girls' school.")

The Library

Remember when I told you that the most underrated, most neglected, most important part of any shop is a good library? Well, I wasn't kidding. I don't know how many letters I've gotten over the years from guys about to start, or even in the middle of restoring an old tractor, asking questions even dumber than the ones I've asked. I'd respond something like, "Haven't you looked at the transmission chapter in your I & T shop manual?" or "Isn't that clearance information provided in the operator's manual for that tractor?" or "Wouldn't that number be in your parts book for that machine?" but it's clear that the question is so dumb, they can't possibly have an I & T shop manual, operator's manual, or parts book. So, I usually just mutter, "Well, you big dummy, I'll bet you weren't doing your homework when you flunked out of the sixth grade either, right?"

I cannot imagine taking the gas cap off a tractor without having first studied the I & T (the full name is *Intertec* and I know I & T isn't the right abbreviation for it, but that's what they call 'em, even on the manuals themselves) shop manual, operator's manual, and parts book for that tractor if they are at all available, and you'll be surprised how many tractors are covered by these absolutely essential references. If you don't own this booklet for your tractor, don't bother anyone else for information because you haven't done your part yet. So why should they do it for you?

Intertec manuals are available from the publisher as well as many retail dealers (listed in Appendix C), many others listed in tractor restoration magazines, journals, and newsletters. They are slim volumes and not cheap—the I & T manual for my Allis WC costs $18 but it would be cheap at three times that cost. I & T shop manuals are meticulously accurate, detailed, wonderfully illustrated guides to disassembling, repairing, and restoring tractors. For a novice like me, the language is sometimes complicated and arcane; I never understood the description or the illustrations of how to overhaul shifters until I had already overhauled a shifter. I'm not sure anyone ever could describe something that complicated with the English language or with line drawings. But most of the language is clear, and if you can't understand it, just go to town and ask some of your human resources.

But be prepared: my ears are still burning from the time I went into the tavern and casually asked several mechanic-sorts sitting around, "Uh, I'm working on timing my Allis and I'm plowing through the shop manual. Anyone have any idea what TDC could possibly mean?" I could tell from the shouted, choral response and the hoots of laughter that I had just asked a question any ten-year-old kid who had spent more than a week on a farm should be able to answer.

"Top dead center," they yelled in unison.

"BTC?"

"Before top dead center!!"

Embarrassing, yes, but if it weren't for my I & T manual, I wouldn't even know "TDC."

Operators and parts books are available for a lot of old tractors, even though the machines haven't been produced for a half century. You might be able to obtain an original copy of these, but the fact of the matter is, original publications are antiques and are probably worth more as old books than as shop references. Most commercially available copies are photocopies, but since you are interested in information, not old paper, it makes no difference. In fact, the copies are sometimes clearer than the originals. More about that shortly. In Appendix C I've listed some sources for operators and parts manuals.

Operators manuals include service information and procedures for starting, running, storing, and maintaining your machine that might not be available elsewhere, and that aren't always a matter of common sense. There are grease fittings on the Allis WC, for example, tucked deep inside the transmission where you are not likely simply to run across them. The operators manual told me where to look for them and how to get at them.

I bought my parts manual for the Allis WC at the same auction sale of an Allis Chalmers dealer's shop where I met Wayne and Kevin Hilder. Again, it wasn't cheap—$60—but I cannot for the life of me imagine operating without it. A parts book shows an exploded view of every component of the tractor—every component, every nut and bolt and pin!—names them (which is really important for a novice like me who simply doesn't know the names for most of those things), and—this is important—provides the parts numbers for each of those nuts, bolts, and pins. The implication of all that is that I can drop a note to Wayne Hilder or give him a call, as I did this morning, and tell him I need a set of mainshaft roller bearings #211537 and a mainshaft roller bearing spacer #202868 for an Allis WC and in minutes he can tell me if he has it in stock, if he can get it, and how much it will cost.

If you can't buy an old parts book, new copies are available for many tractors (try the same addresses, listed in Appendix C) or, if you have a friendly dealer, perhaps you can ask him to copy his parts book for you. Believe me, if he charges you thirty dollars for a thirty-page parts book, it'll still be worth it, especially if you intend to work on more than one tractor of the model of your heart.

My shop library is a set of shelves under a piece of plywood attached to the wall, slanting down, a light overhead, so I can walk from my tractor to the desk, flip open my manual or parts book and quickly find the information I need. But here's a hint, one of the smartest things I did when I started this whole tractor madness: I dismantled my I & T manual, inserted each page in a commercial plastic sleeve (I got mine from Quill, PO Box 94080, Palatine, IL 60094-4080, 800/789-1331) for about fifteen cents each/, there are cheaper and more expensive ones, depending how heavy-duty they are, but these plastic sleeves are available from any office supply house), and put them in a heavy-duty ring binder (purchased at the same place).

I photocopied my old parts book from the auction sale and inserted those pages in plastic sleeves in a ring binder too. And the operator's manual. I have done this with all my tractors (I also have an Allis C and an International 300). I did it for instruction sheets for my welder, the cornpicker, and a couple other tractors like the WD, which is close enough to the WC to be frequently useful. I clearly marked the ring binders on the outside so I can grab them quickly off the shelf.

What this means is that I can flop open the binder to the page I need, paw through it with greasy, filthy hands, even mark on the page with a grease pencil, without damaging the original page under the plastic. Every so often I take a little soap and water and clean off the plastic, and my shop manual is as good as new. As I said, it's one of the best things I've ever done in my shop.

If I were writing this book for Playboy Publications, no kidding, I would at this point make a point of the importance of Motorbooks International publications. Before I exchanged my first letter with the editorial offices of MBI, as I index it in my library, I was buying that publishing house's books to the point of Linda's distraction. Robert Pripps's *How to Restore Your Farm Tractor* is indispensable for anyone who intends to "do" a tractor. Randy Leffingwell's *The American Farm Tractor* is my dream book. I study C. H. Wendel and Andrew Morland's *Allis Chalmers Tractors* so hard I have to remind myself to blink now and then.

I made such a fuss one night in bed, Linda thought I was throwing a fit, but actually, I had just read in a catalog that, at the very time I was struggling with my own magneto problems, MBI was going to release a new book on precisely that problem, Neil Yerigan's *How to Restore Tractor Magnetos*. I could not believe my good fortune, that there actually was about to be a book about the most troublesome, complicated part of any tractor engine (along with the carburetor, and I am hoping it won't be long before MBI helps us out with that, too). Write for a Motorbooks International catalog and make it your wish list for next Christmas. Or your birthday. Or, if you are really a brave man, for your anniversary.

Most of the rest of my shop library is made up of catalogs, but don't laugh—it's not just a matter of looking for parts and tools and spending money. Catalogs are terrific references for the beginner. I save myself a lot of embarrassment with those catalogs. I don't have to go up to town and ask, "Hey, buddies, any of you have one of those little clamper jobbies that look like hose clamps except a lot bigger that you use to squinch down the ringie-thingies so they'll fit around the piston top things that sit on the end of the connector piece that runs from the big, horizontal zigzag shaft up into the vertical round hollow tube?"

With a catalog, the night before you go on a borrowing, begging, or snooping expedition, you thumb through the pages until you find just what it is you need, and there it is—"piston ring compressor." You can go up to town the next day, fully confident that you won't sound like a complete idiot.

The other side of the coin is then possible, when your generous friend says, "I suppose you'll need a ring expander then too, right?"

"Well, I'll have to check and get back to you tomorrow," you say, knowing that you can open up your catalog again that night and get some idea of just what the hell a ring expander looks like.

The fact of the matter is, as I have confessed before, I'm a newcomer to this business. One of the reasons I wasn't using a valve spring compressor when I put this dent in the middle of my forehead is that I didn't know there was such a thing. It was in thumbing through a tool catalog that I spotted a page with several varieties listed and, having had some experience dismantling a valve-in-head engine, could see right away how these things work and how delightful they could be the next time I hunched over an engine head. So, I don't just turn to my catalogs when I need something, because often I'm not even smart or experienced enough to know what it is I need. I have to read the catalog to find what I need.

Parts catalogs are useful not only for buying parts but also for establishing approximate costs of parts before you go to a salvage yard, farm sale, dealership, or parts store, or buy a whole tractor for parts, for that matter. There's no sense in me paying Jim Stromp $75 for a well-used, questionable magneto, for example—except for the good stories I'll probably get from him and the fact that I owe him—if I can buy a fully reconditioned one for $95 and postage. On the other hand and this example is not just theory—it was from a catalog that I found out that I could buy a whole tractor engine with salvageable sleeves and pistons from Jim for the same price it would cost me to buy one new sleeve and piston from most parts catalogs.

Finally, catalogs (and a lot of experience) will help you if you ever find yourself in the pleasant situation of entertaining the sale or bartering of some parts. You'd hate to make the mistake of trading a $100 carburetor for a $3 steering knuckle, for example, or sell an $85 water pump for $10. You don't want to gouge anyone—especially yourself.

I have listed some specific catalogs I use in the Appendixes below, but these are just the mailing lists I have accidentally wound up on. You may have none of the ones I use, a pile of ones I don't, and be perfectly happy and successful. In fact, drop me a note if you have some good ones I don't have. I'm always ready to add more to the bedside pile.

Remember those loose-leaf notebooks and plastic sleeves I use for my shop manuals and parts catalogs? I dismantle all the little instruction and parts books that come with major tools and equipment and give them the same treatment—welder, compressor, grinders, pullers, reamers, that sort of thing. The appropriate use and maintenance of these things is not always obvious and once in a while I find myself needing to go back through the manuals and tech sheets to sort something out. Those times always come when I am slathered fingernails to earlobes with grease, solvent, and sweat, so I have never regretted the extra expense of putting these documents between plastic sheets.

My shop is too dirty for nice books I want to keep nice. Charles Wendel's *The Allis Chalmers Story* is reference work but it is too expensive to stick out in my shop. And there's nothing in it I need very often. Except the listing of the manufacturing dates for various serial numbers of the Allis Chalmers WC. Easily solved: I just made a photocopy of that one page from the book, put it in a plastic sleeve, and posted it on the wall of the shop. That way I can read the book with appropriate reverence whilst in the bosom of my family but have access to the necessary information in it whilst wallowing in my shop.

An important adjunct to my shop and bedside libraries is our bathroom. I keep a supply of parts and tools catalogs there, right beside the throne, and other tractor books that calm the bowels as well as the soul. At the moment, I am lounging my way (it is called a restroom, after all) through C. H. Wendel's *Nebraska Tractor Tests since 1920* and, also by Wendel, *Encyclopedia of American Farm Tractors*. Great literature.

Chapter Seven

Breaking Loose—A Happy Lad at Work in His Shop

◆

I have mercifully forgotten where I first saw those mad, crazy words in print, but I'll never forget the moment: I was reading everything I could about some problem or another, utterly baffled by the mechanical mystery I was examining. Utterly stymied, I turned to the experts and opened a book that surely had the answer for me. And there they were: "Once the unit cover is removed from the cast housing, processes for removal of the various components will be self-evident." I tell you, I about spit. I had no mechanical experience or training, but on the other hand I'm no dummy. In fact, I like to think I even have some innate mechanical skills. But nothing inside that grimy

Roger's Simple Guide to Carburetor Adjustment
From Successful Farming, February 1994

Mel Grim up at the Sinclair station isn't afraid of anything; he'll take on any automotive task. At least that's what I used to think. And then I asked him to work on a carburetor.

"I don't do carburetors," he said, obviously embarrassed.

"Why don't you do carburetors?"

"Just don't."

"Why?"

"Don't."

Turns out, Mel is afraid of carburetors. But that's okay, because so is almost everyone else. One of the things that has surprised me as I have learned ever more about tractor repair and restoration is how timid everyone seems to be about carburetors. Well, I'm not afraid of carburetors. And by the time I get through with you, you won't be afraid of carburetors either.

It's as simple as this: a carburetor mixes air and fuel. It has two little adjusting screws; one is for tuning the fuel/air mixture when the engine is at idle, the other for the engine running at full power. Anyone who knows anything about engines and carburetors will be able to tell you which is which on your particular model, although you'll probably be able to figure it out for yourself just by turning the needles a little in each direction while the machine is running.

Let's take a look at this carburetor on one of my Allis WCs. Hand me that screwdriver. While the engine is at idle, I'll fiddle with this screw until the tractor runs smoothly. Then, while the engine is running at good speed, I dink around with the other screw until the engine runs well there, and that's pretty much all you need to know about carburetor adjustment. The job is done. Does that sound like the kind of thing that strikes terror into the hearts of strong men? I guess not.

Whoops. I guess we must have shaken something loose because you'll note that little drop of gas has formed on the bottom of the carburetor casting. Easy enough. Just tighten this little nut the idle adjustment screw goes through and...well, as luck would have it, that makes it leak a little worse. Let's shut the engine off and take a look at this. It's no big deal, believe me.

We'll need to take the carburetor off, because I think the float needs adjustment, which is what is giving us the gas drip. No problem. Remove the two nuts holding the carburetor to the bottom of the manifold. Whoops. Hey, breaking off a bolt like that is a standard part of tractor work, believe me. We'll get back to that in a minute, but in the meantime, let's look at what's going on inside the carburetor.

Whoa, did you see that little spring fly out of there? Never saw that before. It must have been the culprit. Probably wasn't holding the float right or something. It went over in this direction, can't have gone far. Ouch. The spring must have been a little on the tired side to flatten out like that when I hardly even stepped on it with my full weight. Well, Mel will probably have one something like it in his spare parts box. We can check tomorrow when we go to town for a carburetor gasket.

For the moment, then, let's take a look at that broken manifold bolt. Drilling it out and replacing it requires removal of the entire manifold, which is no more complicated than it appears. The manifold is held onto the engine block by eight studs with brass nuts. Take the nuts off and the manifold comes right off. Whoops.

Whoops. Whoops again. Don't worry: I've never seen anyone take a manifold off without breaking a stud or two. Or three. All you do is take a drill and bit, drill a little hole precisely in the center, take an EZ-Out or any of the dozens of similar extraction devices, screw it backwards into the little hole, and turn firmly with a wrench. Here, I'll show you the process.

Whoops. We've broken off the extractor, a bit more of a problem since an extractor has the hardness of a banker's heart and you're not going to drill it out with whatever you have. We'll have to get that engine uptown somehow and have a mechanic blow it out with a cutting torch. Trust me: It'll only take a few minutes.

The rods inside the holes from the manifold? Those are the valve stems. Why are they all covered with oil and crud? Hmmm. It looks like we're going to have to remove the head and have those valves worked on. (In order to remove the head, you can easily see, you have to take off the water pump first. That's the thing with the fan blades on it. Just three bolts and it's free. And I guess to get the pump off this tractor, you also have to remove the radiator. Whoops. Don't worry about that. We can get it fixed later.)

Look at this! Whoever worked on this tractor last stopped up a leaky pan gasket with window putty. Real bright guy. See, it comes right off! And look at the oil run out. Yuk. If you're going to do something, might just as well do it right, so we'll drop the pan and put a new gasket on. And to do that, looks like we have to take off the steering shaft. Whoops. Ouch. I don't think that's going to need stitches, is It?

Well, maybe we'll have better luck with the oil pan. Hand me that speed wrench and ratchet. Whoops. Well, since we have to take the block up to the mechanic, it won't be any more of a problem to have him take out the broken pan and water pump bolts too. See how everything is starting to dovetail here?

Well, no, the pistons shouldn't shake around in there like that, and now that you mention it, neither should the front wheels and the drive shaft. We'll have plenty of time because we're going to have to order a full set of gaskets anyway, which sometimes takes a few weeks. (Isn't that just the way it goes? If we had *tried* to get a little washer like that to fall through that tiny hole into the water jacket, it would have taken us hours. Maybe when the mechanic is working on the broken studs, he can fish the washer out with a magnet, or something.)

What the heck, while we're at it, let's take a look at the clutch, transmission, and final drive. Complicated? Nah. You'll run into a lot of guys who are afraid of tearing into a transmission or final drive. All they can talk about is how difficult it is to deal with bull gears, the great big hunks of iron at the back wheels. Bull gears are simple mechanics just like everything else on this tractor: if you use common sense and patience, and buy your Liquid Wrench in sixty-gallon drums, none of this is impossible.

All you have to do to get to the bull gears is remove the wheels, which are held on by another set of studs—these threaded rods. Whoops. Boy, that's liable to be a little tough getting back in there. Whoops. Ouch. Did you see where that clip went? Whoops. *There* it is. Well, that should heal up by next week, and I'm right-handed anyway. No problem.

Maybe while we clean up the mess (any good solvent will handle both blood and gear grease or, as is more common, a blend of the two), we can take another look at that carburetor.

Whoops.

iron box was "self-evident." Nothing.

At least not at that moment. And this takes us back to John Jerome and his book *Truck* because that's where the staring comes in. The fact of the matter is, almost everything inside your tractor, from the steering mechanism to the transmission, all through the engine, with the exception of the magneto and carburetor—which no one understands—is self-evident if you take your time, think about it, stand, and stare. One thing I have learned from writing is that our minds don't sleep. When you cash it in for the night, you shut your eyes, but you don't shut your ears, right? Sounds keep right on going in your brain, even if the main switch is turned to "off."

Same thing with your brain. It slows down and kicks back a little but it's not like you're dead. I don't know how often I've gone to bed thinking about a mechanical problem on a tractor, read a little about it in a manual or shop guide, and dozed off...only to sit straight up in bed sometime during the night, saying, "I've got it, I've got it!" Once I've gotten Linda calmed down and assured her that no, it wasn't my youth I've rediscovered, I find that I have actually come up with an answer to my problem while I was sleeping.

So, don't rush. You don't need to take care of every problem with this tractor all at once. Give your head a chance. There's a lot to be done, so work on something else for a while. Let the penetrating oil soak in (into the tractor, not your head). Give the parts some time to dry out. Give your brain some time to percolate. Instead of bullheadedly pounding away at that stuck bolt in the steering pedestal, spend your next couple shop sessions getting those valves cleaned up. You might be surprised how easily the bolt comes out the next time you address it. Faced with precisely this problem right now, I spent all of yesterday fooling around taking stuck rings off a broken piston. It was a pleasant, harmless pastime that gave me time to think and cool down.

My biggest problem with such things has been the kindness of friends. Ol' Dan Selden comes drifting by the shop and takes note of what I'm up to. "Still working on those manifold lugs, I see," he says.

"Yep, and just keep your hands off the wrench," I reply.

"Here. Just let me give it a little tug."

"It's fine. It's on my list for next week."

"Maybe if I turn it back in a tad—UH!—and then back out—UH!...and, I'll be darned. Boy, Rog, that thing must have been pretty rotten to bust off inside the head like that."

Yeah, right, Dan. Next time I'll remember to hide the wrenches when you come in. I'll get that blasted broken lug out of there, all right, but you just added a day to my job by pushing too hard to save me ten minutes.

Curiously, the bulk of the work I wind up doing in my shop with old tractors is precisely that—getting things loose: stuck nuts, stuck bolts, stuck pins, stuck valves, stuck gaskets, stuck gears, stuck screws, stuck fittings, stuck pistons, stuck rings, stuck keys, stuck rods, stuck springs, stuck bearings, stuck seals, stuck shafts, stuck levers, stuck caps, stuck covers, stuck joints... I know it sounds crazy, but about ninety percent of rebuilding an old tractor is unsticking things. Now, I've told you about Mel Grim's trick of using plenty of penetrating oil and tapping the part, and Big Don Hochstetler's adjunct of tapping the part into which the stubborn part goes, but just as there is a world of things to get stuck, there is a world of ways to unstick them.

A fairly standard litany for such a problem would be the following:

1) I twist off the head of a stuck bolt running through the frame and into the cast-iron steering pedestal.

2) Initially I apply hot, lubricating words in hopes of loosening the remains of the bolt through divine intervention.

3) That failing, I douse the stub of a bolt with penetrating oil (in this case, Kroil, recommended by a friend whose almost religious fervor for the penetrant convinced me to try it) and let the problem sit for a week.

4) Returning sometime later, I use a brass punch to bang on the broken bolt a few times. The stub is too short to grasp with Visegrips, so maybe the heat and friction of a left-handed bit and reversible drill will break it loose. I tap a slight divot in the middle of the bolt with a center punch and drill a small hole in the middle of the bolt. (Too big a hole might cause the walls of the bolt to expand too easily outward, more tightly into the threads of the front pedestal.) With a syringe (you can buy nice big ones at a veterinarian's office for a few cents) I squirt penetrating oil into the hole in the bolt so it can soak forward into the threads. I tap the bolts with the punch and stare at the bolt while drinking a beer.

5) A week later I return, tap on the broken bolt, tap in an EZ-Out, already convinced it won't work, and it doesn't. (Me, I believe not in just a second chance but even a 200th chance!) I start the enormous job of trying to take the frame rail off the tractor, thinking maybe I can weld a nut on the broken bolt, if the stub is long enough, and then turn it out with a socket wrench.

All this time there is a kind of dance going on, me circling the tractor, working on this part, working on that, but all the while eyeing that blasted broken bolt, trying to will it out of its rusty hole. I don't know if it does any good, but think how good I'm going to feel when that blasted thing does break loose!

6) When I get the frame off the front-end casting, I find the stub isn't long enough to weld a bolt on. I drill a little larger hole through the bolt. More heat, more pressure, more penetrating oil, more tapping. Nothing. I try heating the bolt and the cast-iron around it, then squirting some cold

water into the hole in the bolt, thinking maybe I can break the rust loose with differential temperatures. Great theory. Doesn't work.

7) I drill the hole a little larger, more oil, tapping, turning. I break out my carbon arc torch and heat the whole area up until the bolt is red hot. I try to turn it out hot. Not a hint of movement. I heat it up again and cool down the bolt. Oil, tapping, pressure. Nothing. I worry about using the carbon arc torch on jobs like this because it's possible the carbon can weld the broken stub in its hole. At this point, it's worth a try, but I keep the torch work as brief as possible.

8) I have now spent nearly six hours trying to break loose ONE stuck bolt. A waste of time? Not unless you call the whole process of spending lots of money and time making an old tractor run a waste of time. It's problem-solving, like a crossword or jigsaw puzzle. If it challenges an old man's brain and lifts an old man's heart, then it's anything but a waste of time.

We are getting close to the end game now. Not many alternatives left. I try two more bits, each a trifle larger than the last. Now there's not much left of the bolt to tap on, nothing for an EZ-Out to grab. I continue squirting penetrant into the hole.

Okay, that's it. There is nothing left to do but drill with the largest bit I have that fits easily within the threaded hole without damaging the threads. The ideal is to drill a hole so precisely sized and centered that it cuts out as much of the bolt as possible while just barely skimming the tops of the threads. And I come pretty close to that ideal. My hole is slightly off center so I nick the threads pretty good on one side but it doesn't look too bad.

With a small chisel and light hammer, I begin tapping at the very slight ridge of bolt still sticking above the front-end casting, trying to knock the shred of the bolt away from the threads, into the middle of the hole. And it works. Slowly but surely the remnants of the bolt collapse into the hole as I tap the chisel around the edges. I hook onto the shreds with needle-nose pliers and zip, there it is. That damned bolt that has been vexing me for months slides from its hole. Talk about the joy of victory!

I run a chase in and out of the bolt hole a few times and rinse out the dirt and bits of metal left in the hole with kerosene. I turn in one of the undamaged bolts which I have also cleaned up with a wire brush, chase, and kerosene, and I am absolutely ecstatic to find that it fits firmly and evenly in the hole. I have not damaged the threads so much that I'll need to re-tap the hole and use a larger bolt (which would also mean that I'd have to drill a larger hole in the frame rail). The victory is so dramatic and total, I am tempted to save the little shell of the ruined bolt as a trophy. Nah, into the wastebasket with it.

After all, there are plenty of other stuck things to tend to, other victories to savor. I have taken carburetors that seem little more than rusted wads of iron and copper and soaked them for weeks in solvent, eventually salvaging a carburetor that works. When a piston is to be pulled from a sleeve where it has been sitting in one spot for a couple of decades, it is almost a sure bet that the piston will be stuck. And the rings will be stuck on the piston. And the sleeve will be stuck in the block. Muscle, penetrating oil, and hours and weeks of tapping on that piston's top and bottom will eventually work it loose. (Be careful with those pistons, because they may be aluminum and a trifle fragile; I use a piece of wood—usually oak or a foot-long section of four-inch fence post to pound on so I don't damage parts.)

Stuck sleeves take a lot of muscle and a sleeve puller, which you can make, have made, or borrow; commercially manufactured ones are awfully expensive for the small shop tractor worker. My puller was made for me by Plumber Dan. It's a hunk of four-and-a half-inch iron pipe, welded shut at one end, a hole drilled in the center of the plug—sort of like a big, iron coffee cup with a hole smack in the middle of the bottom. The cup sits inverted over the sleeve, on the block. A length of one-inch threaded stock goes through the hole in the puller and down through the sleeve. A four-and-a half-inch circle of 3/8" steel with a hole in the middle, like a giant washer, fits over the threaded stock under the sleeve. A nut is tightened on top of the pipe above the block, generating terrific force—and it takes terrific force to break loose a sleeve. This is always a little scary for me because there is a lot of pressure involved, and a lot of dollars. Sleeves are not cheap, and I am always worried about damaging them.

My favorite part of this operation, however, is cleaning pistons, largely because what this job requires is patience, and, while I am not thought of as a patient man, I do have more patience than money. I love sitting at my workbench, cleaning away years of burnt carbon, dirt, and oil, gently coaxing the rings loose in their grooves. Rings, for all the pounding they take during their trillions of trips up and down in those sleeves, are very fragile critters. You can't pry them loose; they will snap off, and while they're not as expensive as sleeves, rings are not cheap. I have had very good luck scrubbing the pistons clean, the rings still stuck in their grooves, with kerosene or solvent. (I like mineral spirits, but be sure you have good ventilation in your shop if you are using this stuff; I have a small exhaust fan immediately on the other side of my bench, so fumes are pulled away from me and out of the shop.) Then I use a dental pick to clean the edges of the rings, without prying at them. Then I gently tap the rings with a neoprene hammer. (I have also used a piece of oak, a sawed-off hammer handle, and a rubber hammer for this job and they worked just fine.)

Eventually you'll see a little kerosene squeezing out the sides of the rings near the ring gap, and then the rings actually begin to give and work loose. I continue tapping lightly all around the ring, rinsing the grooves out frequently with kerosene. Tap, tap, tap, rinse, rinse, rinse, whistle while you work.

Before long—before too long anyway—the rings are completely loose and I can begin cleaning the groove with a groove cleaner, piece of broken ring, or a dental tool, revolving the ring around the piston as I clean or removing the ring altogether. And then another ring, another, another, and there it is, an old piston turned into a bright and shiny part, ready to be put back to work (if it isn't too badly worn).

So, why am I telling you about removing and cleaning a piston and not, say, a PTO transmission? That job has its special problems and pleasures, after all. There's every reason to believe you'll have to do that little task too. Well, when you come right down to it, all of the jobs associated with rebuilding an old tractor are pretty much the same, and every old tractor is pretty much the same too. That's not to say they don't each have their own personalities, advantages, handicaps, quirks, and surprises. They do. Every WC I've opened up has been a new crossword puzzle, with a whole new set of clues and a whole new set of solutions. The general idea of the processes is the same.

So, you'll need your I & T shop manual, and maybe an operators manual and parts manual, for your specific tractor, but the mindset you carry into your project is going to be a lot like that of every other old tractor mechanic you'll meet. That's why you're going to find yourself laughing and exchanging addresses and information with every other old tractor nut you run into, even if you are a card-carrying-two-cylinder John Deere man and your new friend is an industrial-grade Allis Chalmers creeper freak.

He'll have a "secret" penetrant sure to break loose those stuck pistons of yours and he will sooner or later remember some guy he ran into—I think it was at an auction sale in Cedar Grove, Iowa—where the John Deere dealer from—as I recall, it was Amana—picked up six belt pulleys, still in their original boxes. In return, you'll pass along the name of a fellow near your home who specializes in repairing old Allis magnetos, and buddy, you have a friend for life.

Shadetree Genius

From Nebraska Farmer, *"The Liar's Corner," October 1994*

For the first time in my mechanicking career, I worked last week on timing a tractor, Silent Orv, the tractor I've been working on for a year. (Orv has since been rechristened "Roarin' Orv.") Mick "The Brick" Maun and I struggled with the thing the better part of a day, joined later for a few hours by Plumber Dan Selden. If you don't know what timing a tractor ignition involves, it ain't easy. You've got to crank the engine until the valves are just right on the first cylinder and line up a little F on the flywheel with a little mark, and then you align some gears in the magneto (one way for clockwise drives, another for counterclockwise) and ease it up to the impulse, and...well, it's complicated.

But being good boys, we did everything just right. We opened the inspection port in the top of the clutch housing and lined up that blasted F a thousand times while we dinked with the magneto and carburetor. Then we dragged the tractor a hundred yards, opened everything again, and started at point A all over again. Finally, glory of glories, Silent Orv started and ran for the first time in decades. I suppose it sounded like a horribly out of tune engine to passersby, but to me it was like music from a prize-winning symphony orchestra. Beautiful! We opened the champagne, toasted Roarin' Orv, and listened to that engine until it ran out of gas.

That evening, in bed, I thought I'd review the process a little, so I opened up the Allis WC tech manual to the section on magnetos and timing. "Line up the F on the flywheel with the center of the inspection port on the bottom of the clutch housing..."

"Bottom?" *"Bottom*?!" "The port on the BOTTOM of the clutch housing?!!!" We had mis-set the flywheel exactly 180^0 wrong! You can't get more wrong than that. And it still runs! When I told Kenny Porath, master mechanic, what had happened, he said, "Yep, those old tractor engines are pretty forgiving." Buddy, "forgiving" ain't the word for it! I can hardly wait to see how that engine runs when we do the job halfway right!

Believe me, that is not a stretch of the imagination. Linda, Antonia, and I once took a week's vacation in Cancun on the Yucatan peninsula of Mexico. We were on a small sailboat out in the ocean, headed for a reef, where the twenty or so passengers were going to snorkel for exotic fish. I mean, you can't be much further from Dannebrog, Nebraska, a smelly tractor shop, and the innards of an Allis Chalmers WC than that! I was hanging onto the deck of this little cork bobbing in the middle of the ocean and I exchanged a few pleasantries with the young fellow next to me. Seems he was an Illinois farmer, taking a vacation with his wife of only a couple years. Allis Chalmers? Why, he and his father had been farming with ACs for three-quarters of a century! And those WCs, what a machine! And we launched off into a couple hours of Allis WC stories.

Somewhere along here I turned to say something to Linda and Antonia, and my new friend turned to speak to his wife. The women were incredulous—a beautiful day like this, sailing on a turquoise-blue sea, and actually finding some guy to talk tractors with?!

The process of everything from rebuilding a transmission to replacing an oil pan gasket is the same:

1) Look the problem over carefully. Take your time. Clean the part as well as you can with scraper, scrubber, wire brush, solvent, and rag so you can see the problem as clearly as possible. The whole mechanical situation should be shiny.

2) Do your homework. Read everything you can find before you tear into this thing. Do as much as you can to understand what is in there before you open it. Avoid surprises. If possible, get a backup unit, maybe another engine or magneto or whatever you're working on, that is nothing but junk; dismantle it and see what you can see, learn what you can learn. Take another look at the books once you've taken it apart.

3) Haul the parts up to the local tavern, cafe, garage, grain elevator, park bench, or a neighboring farmer and ask the right questions, or see if what you have concluded is anywhere close to the truth. Don't presume that you can see or guess everything; who would have guessed, for example, that you need to tap the lip of an Allis oil pan up a little so it seats well with the block, or that those impossibly long crankshaft end gaskets need to be that long and shouldn't be cut, or that the gaskets should be soaked in water overnight before you put them on the pan, or that you should tighten the pan bolts only enough that the gasket moves slightly rather than pooches out? I wouldn't have, but those things are all good advice. Don Hochstetler told me all that, however, when I told him one evening at Eric's Tavern I was planning to put the oil pan back on The Giltner the next day.

4) Take care as you dismantle anything to keep the parts clearly in order and neatly organized. Don't count on your memory. Write things

Spring in the Air

From Natural History, *"Science Lite," January 1994*

As I understand it, scientists watch for natural patterns and then try to determine exactly how they work and what they mean. Not that scientists are the only people capable of spotting bits and pieces of these patterns, which are often widespread and constant. Take gravity, for example. Not easy to miss gravity. After all, it's not as if Newton *invented* gravity. Cave dwellers had to deal with gravity. Trilobites had to deal with gravity.

Recently I've had to deal with springs (boing-boing springs, not trickle-trickle springs). Springs have suddenly and dramatically inserted themselves in my life. Like the troglodyte or trilobite contemplating gravity, I have had the uncomfortable problem, therefore, of sensing a pattern without being able to pin it down. See what you can do with my raw data and maybe someday they'll name a syndrome after you.

It all started one morning when I was in my shop working on a tractor transmission. I studied the technical manual in detail, I looked at the housing, levers, gears, and rods carefully and from every angle. I was proceeding slowly and cautiously. The problem is, when it comes right down to it, I don't know anything about mechanical things, so in my case all of those precautions are bottom-line necessities.

Whoever wrote technical manuals must have taken his degree in the works of Jean Paul Sartre. Nothing is obvious, even when it appears to be obvious. My suspicions were aroused by the line in the manual that said, "Be careful not to lose the detente spring and ball." Maybe I was tipped off because the statement seemed clear and straightforward. Right—don't lose the detente spring and ball. Made sense to me. But hey, wait a minute. In the chapter on engines, the book doesn't say, "Don't lose the pistons," even though pistons are fairly important components in an engine. I know *that* much about mechanical things. So why go through the trouble of mentioning that I shouldn't lose the detente spring and ball? For that matter, what are detente springs and balls?

I looked at the accompanying diagram. An arrow numbered forty-six pointed to the general direction of precisely where I was working in the transmission. Number forty-six in the list said "detente spring and ball." I checked the book's index; nothing about detente springs or balls. So far, so good. I used a little mirror on a flexible handle to see if I could find anything resembling a spring and ball. Nothing. It had to be inside something else, maybe behind the shaft. I eased the shaft out a little further. Still nothing. I slid the shaft another quarter of an inch.

And then it happened. I heard an ever-so-tiny ping and just out of the corner of my eye sensed—I didn't actually *see* it, only sensed it—something very small flying at great speed out of the transmission case, straight out the open window six feet to my right and into the two-foot-high grass. I didn't need the manual to tell me what it was.

I had no more than sputtered, "Well, I'll be dipped in..." when my astonishment was enhanced by the roar of my daughter Antonia riding by my shop window on our riding mower, throwing mangled grass—and presumably one detente spring and one detente ball—in every direction.

I suppose a skeptical spirit would consider all that a coincidence: "Big deal, you lost a spring and ball, it flew out the window, and your daughter ran over it

continued on next page

with a mower. You're not going to get a law of physics out of that, Welsch."
Well, I'm not done with the story.

The next day I went to Kerry's grocery store after picking up the mail, but to my surprise, Kerry hadn't opened yet. I sat on his doorstep waiting almost a quarter hour before he finally came rushing up. Here, *verbatim*, is what he told me:

"Sorry I'm late, Rog. I can't believe my bad luck. I borrowed a lawn sprinkler from Dad yesterday. Of course he asked me if I knew how to use it and of course I told him I'd have to be an idiot not to. You know, it's one of those 'chuck-chuck-chuck-chuck-chuck…sizzle-sizzle-sizzle-sizzle' ones." Pivoting on his right foot, his right arm extended, Kerry imitated a sprinkler jerking step by step in one direction and then quickly sweeping back.

"Well," Kerry continued, "I wanted to adjust it so it would cover the yard but not hit the house, so I was prying away at this little lever thing under the sprinkler head and all at once, PING…" and Kerry's forefinger described an arc I knew all too well. "This spring-thing flew about thirty feet out into the weeds. I just came back from Maurie Flembeck's place, because I heard he has a metal detector. If I don't find that blasted spring before tonight, my dad is going to kill me."

Right. "Just another coincidence." Still not convinced? Later that same day I was talking with my brother-in-law Gary and I told him what had happened to Kerry and me. And he told me about the time he was out in a boat blind with Mick the Brick(layer) waiting for some ducks to come within range. Mick was showing him how you have to depress a little pin inside the chamber of certain shotguns before you can slide the bolt out, and…. See? You've spotted the pattern too. That's right: a ping, a flash of light, and little plunk in the water about thirty feet from the boat.

I called up Mick to see what he had to say about the events Gary had described, and to verify my impression of an immutable pattern and potential law of physics. Mick confirmed Gary's account, but even more to the point, he told me about the time in Marine boot camp when the Drill Instructor was in the middle of a lecture on how to dismantle some weapon or another and said, "Whatever you do, ladies..."—that's the way DIs talk— *"whatever you do,* be sure you keep your thumb on that little slot right in front of the set screw, because if you don't..." and at that point a spring leaped from beneath the thumb of the poor unfortunate sitting next to Mick.

Mick used the very same word Kerry, Gary, and I had used—"ping"—and with his hand he described the lightning arc. Except in this case, since there were no weeds, grass, or water for it to land in, the spring found its way to the ceiling, directly to a twelve-foot long florescent light bulb immediately over the Drill Instructor's head. Mick says that even before some of the little pieces of glass had stopped rocking on the concrete floor, the DI hoisted the miserable miscreant by his collar and dragged him from the building, never to be seen again. "He's probably still carrying buckets of sand from one end of the camp to the other, even these twenty years later," Mick said.

I think it is pretty clear: springs are not simply coils of metal capable of storing small amounts of energy for later release. There is substantial reason to believe, in my opinion, that springs can think. They do think. *Their thoughts, obviously, are consistent...and malevolent.*

Scientists continue to turn their giant telescopes, antennas, and radio telescope dishes toward space, waiting for a sign, a message, a clue that intelligent life exists *out there.*

I predict that sooner or later one of them will be adjusting the digital calibration retainer, or, for that matter, trying to fix a cheap ballpoint pen, and will see the sign, hear the message, or sense the clue he or she had looked for in the inky blackness of outer space: "Ping!" In fact, didn't I read somewhere that that was the last message from the Mars Explorer? "Ping?"

down—"Parts go on the axle: spacer first, then felt seal, then seal holder, lip side to pedestal, then bearing, bearing cup, wheel, then..." You get the idea.

Put those parts in a clearly marked container. I like large coffee cans with lids for large parts, butter tubs and cottage cheese containers for smaller ones. (Cottage cheese containers have the added advantage for me that they fit very nicely in the four-inch cylinders of an Allis WC, so as I clean a sleeve and piston, I stick a cottage cheese container in the hole to keep everything clean.)

I've heard of people using a Polaroid camera to record how things come apart and go together but I don't think I'd like that because the photos just aren't that clear. At least my photos aren't. Of course my handwriting isn't all that great either, but...

5) Take your time. If you are in a hurry, you're already in trouble. Calm down, take it easy, slow down. Don't force anything. Do whatever you can not to break anything. Not only will you want to salvage as many parts as possible, but you may need even a damaged or worn part to help you find a replacement, so don't throw away anything yet.

There's a lot to do on this little job you've taken on. While you're thinking about the problem you've run into, while you're waiting for the penetrating oil to soak in, while you're waiting for Kenny or Don or Al to have a minute to talk with you, work on something else. Clean a valve, replace a grease zerk, scrub an air cleaner, anything. Wasting time like this today may save you time tomorrow.

I keep a running list of everything I want or need to do in the shop, whether it's work on the current tractor project or some other task I need to take care of. This not only helps me get everything done, eventually, but also gives me ideas of what I can do while I'm waiting for other problems to gestate.

6) Stay safe. It is not only a good idea, but fun to use the right tools on any task. But in the case of safety—good jacks, proper stands, adequate lights, warning devices, eye and ear protection, an alert mind—good tools may very well be the difference between life and death. Linda says that if she ever comes out to the shop and finds me lying dead on the floor, she's going to kick the poop out of me before she calls the rescue unit because it's so terribly stupid to get hurt or die doing something that's supposed to be relaxing. I'd argue with her but she's right.

7) Take time to clean things up. I'm anything but a neatness nut—ask Linda—but I've found it to be a matter of survival to take the time to clean up in the shop on a constant basis. The first minutes or hour I spend in the shop are reserved for tucking things away, cleaning up tools and stowing them, sweeping the floor, that sort of thing. It gives me time to think and get in the mood. The last few shop minutes or hour are also given over

to cleaning up—mostly me, but tidying up the shop in general too. It's not simply a preoccupation with cleanliness; it's too easy to lose parts and tools in a messy shop. It's too easy to slip on a tool or patch of grease and get hurt. It's too easy for a fire to start in piles of trash and open containers of volatile liquids.

I also take some pride in my shop. My mother looks at it and sees a real mess. It smells bad, it is not tidy, it is not clean; but it is not a hopeless mess. Far from wishing it messier, I wish it were tidier, and I work toward that goal.

Whenever I have a nice day when it's warm and not too windy, I wrench a day away from working on my tractors to cleaning out my shop. I throw open the doors, sweep, swab the floor with cleaners, hose everything out, shake out the rugs, clean off my bench tops, haul out buckets of aluminum cans, waste metal, and trash. It isn't fun for me, because I would much rather spend time tinkering with my tractors, but when it's all done and I look over the final result, my heart just feels good. The next time I drop a washer and it rolls between my feet and off to the other work bay, and I actually manage to find the thing, I'll thank myself for taking the time to clean things up the week before.

8) Don't make your tractor work a job. Not long ago I went up to the town tavern after a terrific day of playing with my new welder. Boy, I had run beads, and welded joints, and cut stock until I was worn to a frazzle. I was drenched in sweat, dirty and smelly from the smoke and metal, thoroughly exhausted. Man, did I feel good! I climbed onto a bar stool next to a friend who works in a welding shop: "Good grief, Welsch, what have you been doing?" he asked. "You look worse than I do."

"I spent the day welding. What fun! What have you been doing?" I replied.

"I spent the day welding. What a drag!" he said.

The difference is between a hobby and a job, what you want to do and what you have to do; he was working, I was playing. It's possible, if you take this tractor project of yours too seriously, it just might turn into a job, something you have to do, something you have to do in a certain way. It's possible to be so obsessed with one's own standards—or worse, someone else's—that the fun is altogether squoze out of it. It's up to you, of course, but I hope you don't let that happen. Keep on laughing. Do only what you want to do and only as much as you want to do.

9) Don't let anyone else tell you what you should be doing. Take advice, gather information, listen and learn, but if someone tells you that you have completely ruined your tractor because an air cleaner on a 1934 Allis Chalmers WC should be mounted with half-inch square-head bolts and you, cursed dog that you are, have used half-inch hex-head bolts, you have permission to stuff an inch-and-a-quarter US fine-threaded lug stud

up their air cleaner. You just don't have to pay any attention to that sort of thing. Okay, there are obsessive people who wind up with tractors so gorgeous they can't be used, far more splendid than they were when they rolled off the assembly line. If that's what you want, go for it. If you're not particularly interested in that sort of manic behavior, don't bother.

10) And now I'm going to tell you what to do even though I told you not to pay any attention to people who tell you what to do: clean everything before you put it back on the machine. Again, this is not a matter of being a clean freak. If you dismantle and thoroughly clean, for example, a water pump before you put it back on, check its seals and bearings, check its settings and parts, you may be saving yourself even more work down the line. I use this example because I made that mistake once. I did clean the water pump but after reassembling the pump, it leaked water like crazy, right out the rotor. Bad seal. Even I could see that. So, I had to dismantle the sheet metal, radiator, and water pump and do the job I should have done in the first place.

Moreover, clean parts, with clean fasteners, are immeasurably easier to reinstall than greasy, filthy parts and fasteners. I know that sooner or later I am going to dismantle the first two or three tractors I worked on and redo them. I made too many mistakes. I left too many things undone. I did one thing right: I cleaned everything up. When I get around to that job, it will be a joy because I know that everything is going to come apart easily and cleanly.

In my case, I like the cleaning part of tractor work, so it's easy. In fact, it's fun. I hope you feel the same way.

I am surprised when I read in many books on tractor restoration that you may be lucky and find a tractor that still runs, so you won't have to take it apart. Oh, okay, one such book says, maybe you should go ahead and take off the oil pan anyway just to check the oil pump.

Man, if you are going to operate like that, what are you doing working on a tractor anyway? The fun of this whole thing is precisely taking that machine apart, cleaning it up, checking everything, putting it back together, and hearing it run again, better than it was before. I cannot for the life of me imagine getting an old tractor, finding that it runs, taking the dents out of it, painting it, and calling it "restored."

Having said that, again I'll have to confess a little uneasiness on my part. I can very easily imagine a real restorer saying at this point, "Welsch, you dim bulb, what is the sense of doing all that work on a tractor and then not giving it a first-class body work-over and paint job? And then you have the nerve to tell someone else he has to completely disassemble his tractor just because you're a mechanics nut?! You got some gall, pal!"

Uh, well, so's your old lady. Okay, I'm guilty as charged. But I still think you should take apart that PTO transmission and that engine and renew the seals, check the bearings, adjust the settings, all that sort of thing.

11) On the other hand, I said you have only yourself to please, but if you are a dabbler like me, if you don't do everything just right, like a real restorer, try not to do anything that will permanently mar your tractor. Sure, it's your tractor, I said that already too; but you are also dealing with a piece of history, a machine with some dignity of its own, and some potential value—not just financial, I hasten to add—to others. It's one thing to put on a nut or v-belt that isn't anywhere close to what was on the machine originally; it's another to cut into the frame and weld on a battery holder. You can't afford to buy tires historically accurate for your tractor but you want to drive it in the town's Fourth of July parade? Drive that baby on whatever rubber you can put on it. The fun of driving it, the pleasure of those who see you and your machine, will not be diminished because the pattern on your tires isn't historically accurate. Ignore anyone who tells you otherwise, and there are those zealots out there who will tell you precisely that. Remember: there ain't no rules.

12) When you pull that piece of rusting metal out of some farmer's woodlot and take it to your shop for a couple years' worth of attention, you are, in my mind, performing a major service: you are taking junk and making it treasure. You are removing an ecological blight, maybe even a hazard, and making it useful. So, don't botch that beautiful scheme by being careless with solvents, waste oil, old tires, scrap metal, paints, that sort of thing. Dispose of all those things carefully and considerately. Your tractor expects it of you.

Afterword

◆

So, there you have it. That's just about everything I know, or that I knew at the point I wrote it, because for me the real excitement of all this tractor stuff is that I am learning new things every day. That's why I wrote this book, to tell you about all the great things involved in tractor restoration that the tech manuals, how-tos, and step-by-steps don't tell you. To me, the important side of my shop work isn't the repairs I do on my tractors so much as the repairs I do on me.

Yes, there's something to taking a piece of litter out of a woodlot, an eyesore from the back of a barn, a piece of cold, dead junk from a salvage yard, and transforming it into a treasure, a family heirloom, a living piece of machinery. Sure, you may actually make some money on your tractor work (good luck!!) and, as I have done, make a substantial dent in your blood pressure readings. Okay, we can use high-falutin' language and talk about building monuments to agriculture when we are out there in the shop banging away on old iron—tributes to technology, hymns of praise to human ingenuity, yeah, yeah, yeah, blah blah woof woof.

But all those practical and theoretical considerations fade and pale, in my mind, when compared with the romance of the process.

Yes, romance. You greasy lug-nuts probably don't like to think about romance, but by God, it's there. At least for me. I think about the men who bought these tractors and were proud of them, the endless hours they spent sitting on them in the fields, growing food for the world. The disappointment of crops lost, the triumph of crops gained. I wonder about the anxiety they must have felt, spending this much money—in the thirties, for Pete's sake!—on a piece of machinery. I think about the horses that were sold when this machine came into the farmyard.

The goofiest part of my vision, I suppose, is my concern for the feelings of the tractors. And I can hear the hard-headed mechanics among you hooting at that notion. But look here, grease monkey, I've talked with you and listened to you up at the tavern and at the tractor shows. I've read your letters. I've heard what you say about these machines, and that ain't all iron and hardware I hear in your voice. You may not use the words "love" or "respect," you would probably deny any hint of an idea that these old machines have souls, but you don't have to say a word: it's there in your voice. You feel it too. ·

No one feels that way about a television set or power drill. No one talks that way about his electric shaver or air conditioner. You talk about that old tractor of yours the way you talk about a good dog. That's your heart talking, not your mind, you phoney baloney. You don't have to confess your feelings, because they're right there on your sleeve. So, having read this, I hope you understand that there's no need for you to be embarrassed. There are a lot of us who feel the same way. Most of us. Maybe all of us.

I'm not even sure what all the dimensions of tractor restoration are, where all the potential directions lead. So I'll do what I always do—tell another story. Not long ago I was autographing books at a bookstore in a Lincoln, Nebraska, shopping mall. Here were all these admiring fans lined up, bubbling with pre-Christmas enthusiasm, anxious to talk with me, looking forward to my latest book (this one was a book for young readers about Native American culture). My ego was pretty puffed up, as you can imagine.

There was a lull and here come three punk teenagers waltzing along. Jeez. I hate teenagers. These guys are dressed like teenagers, walk like teenagers, talk like teenagers, and there isn't the slightest doubt in my mind but that these bozos are out looking for trouble.

And what do they see in front of them  but a fat old fart pompously signing a book he's written for little kids. Man, what a target! He can't go anywhere, he can't do anything but sit there and take whatever crap we choose to unload on him, I can hear them thinking.

Sure enough, they come right up to my table. "Hi," one of them says off-handedly, "Signing books?" Duh, yeah, I'm signing books. "Huh," one says, sort of elbowing up to the front of the table. He looks at one of the books, thumbs through it. "You're Roger Welsch then?" Duh, yeah, I'm Roger Welsch.

"You the guy with the Allis WCs?"

WHOA! What's this? The kid is talking tractors. MY tractors! He didn't just stumble on me. He's here on purpose.

"You know about Allis WCs?" I ask.

And the kid lit up. From just another cynical, slouching pain-in-the-butt he was suddenly standing straight, beaming, full of life, interested, interesting. Was it just me? Was all this happening in my mind because the boy mentioned tractors?

Not hardly. The young man (notice that he has gone from a "punk bozo" through "boy" to "young man") went on to tell me that he had acquired his grandfather's Allis WC and was about to launch off on the project of restoring it. He talked shyly but enthusiastically with me about the prospect, asked about parts and books, techniques and approaches. And I let everyone else in the line just stand there and wait while I talked with this lad about the obviously promising direction his future was taking.

That night I drove home and gushed to Linda about the experience—and then cursed, "Damn it anyway!"

"What's wrong?" she asked with concern.

"I should have gotten the kid's name and address. There are things I could have sent him, things I could have told him, advice, parts, all kinds of things."

"Would the bookstore know who he was?" she asked.

"No way at all. He's lost, gone, finis. He didn't even buy a book. What an idiot I am."

But what was done was done and there wasn't a single thing I could do to change that fact.

Just a little over a week later, however, our mail included an envelope adorned with bright orange drawings of Allis Chalmers tractors. The letter was from John Sypal, the young man with the WC. It's rare these days for youngsters to show enthusiasm about anything, or to deal on an open and receptive level with old guys like me. And the reverse is true too, after all. In all honesty, I don't exactly make young people welcome in my life.

And there it is. We tractor fanatics may differ drastically in our tastes in music, or politics, or religion, or economic status. Doesn't matter. This love for old tractors has nothing to do with things like that, or with things like whether we grew up on the farm or in a city, or whether we are master mechanics or rank novices. This isn't about money or age, sex or race. Our love for these old machines is what we have in common, and it's all we need.

Mr. Rustoration Answer Man: Restorer, Mechanic, Gear Head, Enthusiast, Tinkerer, or Dabbler

From Successful Farming, *mid-February 1995*

Most of the time, we don't have much doubt about what we are. In fact, people are eager to tell us what we are. "You blooming idiot, what do you think you are, a race car driver?" See, that's pretty clear, isn't it? You may or may not be a race car driver, but there's not much question about being a blooming idiot.

The situation is not all that clear, however, when you work on old tractors. I know I'm not in the class of those who *restore* tractors so they're better looking and running than they were when they came off the assembly line. But I also know I'm a long way from where I was when I first twisted off a manifold lug and figured I'd ruined the engine.

Well, you know by now you can count on me to give important issues like this a lot of serious thought and to share the results with you, and this is the problem I'm going to address this time. There's no longer a need for you to stand there scratching your head when someone asks you exactly what it is you do with old tractors. Take the following handy test in the privacy of your own shop and you will know *exactly* where you stand in the world of tractor rustoration—restorer, mechanic, gearhead, enthusiast, tinkerer, or dabbler.

Answer each of the following questions and record the score of your response in the box to the left of the item; at the end of the exam, total your score, consult the scoring guide, and you will never again have to wonder what you are. And if this test doesn't make it perfectly clear what you are, I'll bet your wife will be glad to tell you any time you have the courage to ask.

Question	Points	Your Score
You know your tractor's:		[ ]
color	1 pt.	
make	2 pts.	
year	3 pts.	
serial number	4 pts.	
rod bearing tolerances	5 pts.	
religious orientation	6 pts.	
You want:		[ ]
a shiny new tractor	1 pt.	
to sell your tractor	2 pts.	
to keep your tractor	3 pts.	
to fix your tractor	4 pts.	
to restore your tractor	5 pts.	
a meaningful relationship with your tractor	6 pts.	
You:		[ ]
used to have a wrench here somewhere	1 pt.	
borrow a wrench when needed	2 pts.	
have a wrench	3 pts.	
own a wrench	4 pts.	
have a full set of sockets, six- and eight-point	5 pts.	
the guy at Sears knows you by your first name	6 pts.	

continued on next page

Your: [   ]
wife complains you never fix anything   1 pt.
wife complains you never fix anything   2 pts.
   important
wife complains   3 pts.
girlfriend complains   4 pts.
you met a girl once but she had the wrong kind
   of tractor   5 pts.
you used to have a wife
around here somewhere   6 pts.

You have grease: [   ]
on your handkerchief   1 pt.
on your shirt cuff   2 pts.
on your nose   3 pts.
under your fingernails   4 pts.
under your toenails   5 pts.
where the sun don't shine   6 pts.

You do your tractor work: [   ]
by watching when the mechanic
changes its oil   1 pt.
in the driveway   2 pts.
under a shade tree   3 pts.
in your car's garage   4 pts.

in your tractor shop   5 pts.
in the kitchen   6 pts.

Your tractor is: [   ]
around somewhere   1 pt.
parked under a mulberry tree   2 pts.
under a tarp behind the barn   3 pts.
in a shed   4 pts.
locked in the shop   5 pts.
in a Swiss bank   6 pts.

You call your tractor: [   ]
it   1 pt.
the tractor   2 pts.
by its manufacturer's name   3 pts.
Big Guy   4 pts.
he   5 pts.
she   6 pts.

Last year your tractor restoration
   expenses were: [   ]
$0   1 pt.
$50   2 pts.

$500	3 pts.
can't say	4 pts.
won't say	5 pts.
still in litigation	6 pts.

You: [   ]

were left your tractor in your grandpa's will	1 pt.
were given it for a lawn decoration	2 pts.
got it at an auction when you scratched your nose	3 pts.
bought it on purpose	4 pts.
paid for it while your wife looked on	5 pts.
traded one of your children for it	6 pts.

TOTAL POINTS   [   ]

There is a potential of sixty possible points. Add up all your points and match your score with the ratings schedule below:

56-60 points = RESTORER FIRST CLASS. Take a look at the Yellow Pages under "Psychiatrists, Emergency Care," *soon*.

51-56 points = RESTORER. Try not to breathe any more solvent fumes.

46-50 points = MASTER MECHANIC. Roosevelt? No, we've had several presidents since then.

41-45 points = MECHANIC. Rumleys? No, they don't make them anymore.

36-40 points = GEAR HEAD. Get your wrench away from that Allis.

31-35 points = GEAR HEAD JUNIOR. No, I don't want to sell my tractor.

26-30 points = ENTHUSIAST. You need a carburetor? Money's no object?

21-25 points = ENTHUSIAST SECOND GRADE. Seen the new Kamikazi S12 tractor? Real shiny.

16-20 points = TINKERER. You wouldn't take $100 for that pile of rust, would you?

11-15 points = APPRENTIC TINKERER. Tell you what, buddy, just 'cause I like your looks, I'll haul that junk outa here for you.

6-10 points = DABBLER. Tell you what, buddy, just 'cause I like your looks, I'll haul that junk outa here for you. For $50.

0-5 points = BEGINNING DABBLER. You know what you need? You need a good tractor. A real classic. And I have just the one for you. Step over here to this shed with me and I'm going to make you the investment offer of your life, young man. What you see here is a rare prize, and just because I like your looks…

I'm going to get myself in some trouble with this, I know, but I have a cousin who keeps trying to get me into his pitch on old tractors—antique tractor pulling contests. The idea is you hook old tractors up to impossible weights and see how far they can move them. That's like taking this old professor and announcing that he's going to have to dig out his old lesson plans and go back to lecturing bored undergraduates and grading 200 papers during Christmas vacation. Nosirree. The tractors at Welsch's Tractor Rest Home will never again feel the strain of the plow or labor in the dirt of the cornpicker. These machines will rest forever, roaring into action only to be admired and respected as fine old machines when I drive into town to show them off.

Tractor Clubs and Associations ♦

I have already acknowledged the generosity and cooperation of Dave Mowitz and *Successful Farming* in this book a couple times, but I need to say it all again because this appendix is pretty much lifted from their work in the pioneering series, *Ageless Iron*, published by that magazine and edited by Mowitz. If they do nothing else in this life, Dave and *Successful Farming* have earned their entry ticket to tractor heaven!

Advance Rumley

The Rumley Newsletter
PO Box 12
Moline, IL 61265
309/764-6753

Rumely Collector's News
12109 Mennonite Church Rd
Tremont, IL 61568
309/925-3932

Allis Chalmers

The Allis Connection
161 Hillcrest Ct
Central City IA 52214

Old Allis News
10925 Love Rd
Bellevue, MI 49021
616/763-9770

B. F. Avery

Tru-Draft Registry (General, Wards
   Twin Row, B. F. Avery, and M-M
   Avery)
109 West Center
Farmersville, OH 45325

Case

J. I. Case Collector's Assn.
Old Abe's News
Rt 2, Box 242
Vinton, OH 45686-9741
614/388-8895

Case Heritage Foundation
PO Box 5128
Bella Vista, AR 72714-0128
501/855-0312

Caterpillar

Antique Caterpillar Machinery Owners
 Club
10816 Monitor-McKee Rd NE
Woodburn, OR 97071
503/634-2496

Cockshutt

International Cockshutt Club
2910 Essex Rd
LaRue, OH 43332
614/499-2961

The Golden Arrow Magazine
N7209 St Hwy 67
Mayville, WI 53050
414/387-4578

David Bradley

David Bradley Newsletter
936 Clarkson Rd.
Vine Grove, KY 40175

Ferguson

Ferguson Club
Sutton House, Sutton
Tenbury Wells
Worcestershire WR15 8RJ
United Kingdom

Ford

Ford/Fordson Registry and Collectors
 Assn
645 Loveland
Miamiville Rd
Loveland, OH 45140

The 9N-2N-8N-NAA Newsletter
154 Blackwood Ln
Stamford, CT 06903
203/322-7283

Gibson

Gibson Tractor Club
4200 Winwood Ct
Floyds Knob, IN 47119-9225

Hart-Parr/Oliver

Hart-Parr/Oliver Collectors Club
Box 685
Charles City, IA 50616

Oliver Collector's News
RR 1 Box 44
Manvel, ND 58256-0044

International Harvester Co.

IH Collectors Association
RR 2 Box 286
Winamac, IN 46996

Red Power Magazine
Box 277
Battle Creek, IA 51006

John Deere

Green Magazine
RR 1
Bee, NE 68314

Two Cylinder Club
PO Box 219
Grundy Center, IA 50638-0219

Massey-Ferguson

Massey Collectors News
Box 529
Denver, IA 50622
319/984-5292

Minneapolis-Moline

M-M Corresponder
3693 M Ave
Vail, IA 51465
712/677-2433

The Prairie Gold Rush
RR 1 Box 119
Francesville, IN 47946

Silver King

Silver Kings of Yesteryear
4520 Bullhead Rd
Willard, OH 44890
419/935-5482

General Interest

Antique Power Magazine
PO Box 1000
Westerville, OH 43081-7000
614/848-5038

Belt Pulley Magazine
PO Box 83
Nokomis, IL 62075
217/563-2612

Early Day Engine and Tractor Assn.
3510 Brooklake Rd
Brooks, OR 97303
717/392-0733Engineers and Engines
2240 Oak Leaf St
PO Box 2757
Joliet, IL 60434-2757

Farm Antique News
PO Box 812
Tarkio, MO 64491
816/736-4528

Gas Engine Magazine
PO Box 328
Lancaster, PA 17608
717/392-0733

The Hook (Pullers Magazine)
PO Box 937
Powell, OH 43065-0937
614/040-5038

Tools and Parts ◆

*T*his sort of information is constantly changing, as suppliers spring up and disappear, change addresses, and add product lines. The people listed below are folks I have dealt with and had good luck with, but absence from this list doesn't imply suppliers might not be reliable. Maybe I just haven't heard about them yet. As I wrote above in the text of this book, I still think your best bet is to get yourself a subscription to the magazine or club, or a bunch of them for that matter, that speaks to your interests; then, read not only the articles but also the advertisements. You will find that there are suppliers who specialize in battery boxes and tires, MinnyMos and Davises, two-pistons and diesels, and you just might find them listed in the pages of the specialty publications. The short annotated list below will give you a start.

Ag Tractor Supply
PO Box 276
Stuart, IA 50250
800/944-2898
 These folks publish a super catalog and have always been cooperative in providing quality, new parts for my tractors. They also list used parts but I've only bought a few. I have found the fellows on the phone to be very helpful and knowledgeable about old tractors. You can also buy I & T shop manuals and tools from this catalog.

Austin Farm Parts
Butler, MO 64730
816/679-4080
 This is no a catalog of parts but a catalog of places where parts can be found, a remarkable directory to hundreds of salvage yards all across the

nation, with some notes as to the kinds of parts or kinds of tractors for which the yards might be especially useful. I imagine that this listing is particularly useful for those of you who are working with rare and unusual tractors, or particularly old tractors, where new parts are out of the question.

CT Farm and Family
3915 Delaware Ave
PO Box 3330
Des Moines, IA 50316
515/266-3101

I don't know for sure, but from the similarities of the catalogs, I'd guess that this is the same reliable outfit at Ag Tractor Supply listed above. I've ordered from both and had great service and products from both.

The Eastwood Company
580 Lancaster Ave
Box 3014
Malvern, PA 19355-0714
800/345-1178

Eastwood specializes in top-notch restoration tools and supplies from welding to glasswork, exhaust to electrical systems. Eastwood is a little priccy but, boy, when you decide you need a really good tool or top-of-the-line supply, Eastwood is a good place to buy it. (This is where I found the Snap-Ups!)

Gempler's
PO Box 270
211 Blue Mounds Rd
Mt Horeb, WI 53572
800/382-8473

Tractor restorers turn to Gempler's for tools and supplies for restoring tires but the catalog also lists other farm and vehicle tools and supplies. This is where I got my great gate signs about guard dogs, manure pits, and dangerous monkeys.

Griot's Garage
3500-A 20th St E
Tacoma, WA 98424
800/345-5789

Griot's Garage is a little like Gearhead Heaven. This slim catalog offers very high-grade restoration tools and supplies. It ain't cheap but when you buy a tool from Griot's you have an heirloom for your grandkids. For example, Griot's set of four three-cam lug pullers is priced right up there with Snap-On; I'd sure love to own a set and probably eventually will spring for one, but it will constitute a real investment. So, I dog-ear the page and tuck it away. Maybe some day...

Harbor Freight Tools
3491 Mission Oaks Blvd
Camarillo, CA 93011-6010
800/423-2567

Despite my love for high-quality tools, I can't always afford them. I have bought a lot of good quality, low-priced tools from Harbor Freight. I dream of replacing them some day with really good stuff, but I don't doubt that when I kick off and my shop tools go on the auction block, there will be plenty of Harbor Freight products for sale, many of them well worn but still with plenty of use in them.

Hemmings Motor News
PO Box 1108
Bennington, VT 05201

I have a hard time thinking of Hemmings as a monthly "magazine" because it runs somewhere around a thousand pages, which is more like a book. A big book! Hemmings is the automobile nut's dream book. It lists everything from antique Cords to slightly used Indy cars and everything you could possibly need to restore absolutely anything. Each issue is almost a thousand pages of single-spaced, small type classified ads, all dealing with vehicles. Until fairly recently Hemmings was restricted pretty much to automobiles and trucks, however, but now there is a modest section devoted to "Tractors, Farm Equipment, etc., For Sale" and "Tractors, Farm Equipment, etc., Wanted." I am assured by the editors they want those sections to expand, and so do I.

Despite the enormous size of this "magazine," it is very cheap (at this writing, less than five dollars), so if you wonder at all if Hemmings might help you, pick up a copy. Even if you don't find what you want, you will spend many happy hours thumbing through it and dreaming of the day when you're just a little tired of working on old International tractors and decide, what the heck, you'd like to roll, say, a 1935 Auburn Model 851 Bobtail Speedster into the shop and give it a whirl. You'll find the car and the parts you need in Hemmings.

J. C. Whitney
1917-19 Archer Ave
PO Box 8410
Chicago, IL 60680
312/431-5625

J. C. Whitney supplies parts and tools for auto repair but many items are, of course, useful for working on tractors. Some of the tools offered by J. C.

Whitney are rarely premium quality, but I have picked up some real bargains—for example, my engine hoist and stand are from J. C. Whitney and are the best I've found anywhere close to the price.

Mack Tools
(check your local phone book under "tools" for an address and phone)

I have tried and tried to make contact with Mack Tools because so many of my friends are fans of their products, but so far I have had no luck. My telephone and phone messages have not been answered.

Nebraska Tractor Testing Laboratory
Dept. of Agricultural Engineering
University of Nebraska—East Campus
Lincoln, NE 68583-0832

The University of Nebraska is *the* place where the world's tractors are tested for consumer information. For a couple dollars, you can obtain a list of all the tractors for which the lab has data and for less than a dollar you can obtain information about your machine. Bargains like this don't come along much any more. My suggestion, if these reports interest you, is to buy *all* of them! Motorbooks International has published C. H. Wendell's compilation of all Nebraska's tractor reports in a beautiful book that I never tire of thumbing through. It is cleverly titled, *Nebraska Tractor Tests Since 1920*.

Sears
Craftsman Power and Hand Tools
20 Presidential Dr
Roselle, IL 60172
800/377-7414

This is where I buy my prize tools. They are not the best but they fall within my financial abilities and are damned fine tools. Unfortunately, Sears has made major concessions to other bozos, the ones who fool around with wood, tin, stuff like that, so this catalog is only useful for tractor workers, and the sections that are useful are far from complete. I find myself often disappointed that I cannot find the tool I need here. But for basic hand tools and basic automotive and tractor tools, this is a great place to start.

Snap-On Tools
2801 80th St
Kenosha, WI 53141-1410
414/656-1403

I don't own a single Snap-On tool. I don't even know how you buy them. I have seen a few at sales, going for premium prices, and in pawn shops, more expensive used than new Craftsman tools, and I have seen the trucks, but I don't know how you buy Snap-On tools. I have thought about stealing a truck and burying it somewhere on my farm so I could play with the tools without fear of being caught, but I have never peered inside one of those mysterious behemoths. Maybe it's the mystery of the things that makes them so expensive.

Somehow, I got hold of a Snap-On catalog, and I have thumbed it darn near to death, however. The tools are beautiful; the catalog is spectacular. Snap-On has eight different regional distribution offices, each accessible through a 1-800 number:

New England (Boston): 800/879-3322

Eastern Seaboard (Philadelphia): 800/926-5544

South-Central (Dallas): 800/756-3344

Great Lakes (Milwaukee): 800/759-8877

Northern Plains (Kansas City): 800/947-7788

Southwest (San Diego): 800/766-4455

Southeast (Atlanta): 800/947-6655

West (Sacramento): 800/865-1199

To get a Snap-On salesman for my small, remote town, I then had to call a state office, where I got a number for my local salesman. Phew, they don't make it easy. I suspect that because their tools are not exactly run-of-the-mill, shade-tree mechanic items, they'd just as soon not bother with us rinky-dink mechanics. Maybe my dealer will stop by some day. I guess when that happens, I'll just sell the farm. But I'll have a bunch of nice tools!

Surplus Tractor Parts
3215 W. Main Ave
PO Box 2125
Fargo, ND 58107
800/859-2045

This parts catalog is the best one I have. STP Corp carries new and used parts for all tractors, no matter how old. Their prices are comparable with CT Farm and Family and Ag Supply so when I need parts, I do some comparison shopping, sorting through all three, checking prices. CT and Ag Supply carry some parts STP doesn't have, and vice versa, so it is worth checking. When I started working on tractors I couldn't believe that you can still buy new parts for a sixty-year-old tractor, but here they are, and at prices that are about the same or cheaper than you pay for that big, fancy, new car of yours.

Operators, Owners, and Technical Manuals

◆

I'm a former professor, so I believe in homework. But for me, it's more than that. I maintain a library of books, papers, and catalogs in my shop for immediate reference while I am working, but I keep a pretty tall pile of these publications at my bedside and in the bathroom too. This is not only fun reading, but often I find that when I have worked all day at a problem in the shop, I will be looking through a tech manual just before I go to sleep, and whoa! there is the solution I have been looking for all day long, right there in the pages of my beddie time reading!

Diamond Farm Book Publishers
RR 3 Brighton, Ontario, Canada
KOK 1HO
I haven't ordered anything from this source but I've heard the catalog is worth sending for.

I & T Shop Service
Intertec
PO Box 12901
Overland Park KS 66282-2901
I feel uneasy about tucking this crucial address deep down among all the others because this address is the most important one in this book. I & T is the source for shop manuals for tractors. Don't turn the first nut on your machine until you have the appropriate I & T shop manual for your tractor in your hands. There are photos, exploded views, illustrations, detailed descriptions, tips, hints, tolerances, all packed into a few pages. I can hear you cheap boogers now: "I'm not about to spend $18 on a pamphlet that's only 100 pages long!" Buddy, this is going to be the cheapest eighteen cents a sheet you've ever spent! Buy two of these—one for the shop, one for the bedroom.

Jensales Company
PO box 277
Clarks Grove, MN 56016
800/443-0625

Warren Jensen offers a wide range of reproductions of antique tractor manuals, over 150 for Allises alone! Three for the WC Allis! These are very high-priced for what is essentially a Xerox copy but they are also very useful—in some cases indisposable—and certainly cheaper than buying an antique original. Jensales also carries I & T manuals.

Motorbooks International
PO Box 2
729 Prospect Ave
Osceola, WI 54020
800/826-6600

I know what you're thinking. And you're wrong. If I were writing this book for any other publisher, I would nonetheless insist on including this publisher under resources because there's no one else even close when it comes to automotive and tractor books. This catalog is in and of itself great gearhead reading, including everything from the fine art of pinstriping street rods to the nuts and bolts of rebuilding antique tractor magnetos, from Indy car driving hints to coffee table tractor books. Randy Leffingwell's *The American Farm Tractor* and Robert N. Pripps' *How to Restore Your Farm Tractor* from this publisher are required reading; if you have an Allis, Deere, Minnie-Mo, Ford, Case, or International McCormick and don't own Motorbooks Farm Tractor Color History volume on your tractor, well, you should be ashamed to call yourself an old-iron nut.

Nebraska Tractor Testing Laboratory
Dept of Ag Engineering
University of Nebraska-East Campus
Lincoln NE 68583-0832

The University of Nebraska is the place where the world's tractors have been tested for consumer information, and these reports are public information. For a couple dollars you can obtain a list of all the tractors for which the lab has data and for less than a dollar you can obtain the information about your machine. Bargains like this don't come along much any more. My suggestion, if these reports interest you, is to buy all of them! Motorbooks International has published C. H. Wendel's compilation of all Nebraska's tractor reports in a beautiful book that I never tire of thumbing through. It is cleverly titled, *Nebraska Tractor Tests Since 1920.*

Successful Farming
1716 Locust St
Des Moines IA 50309-3023

Because of the dedication of machinery editor Dave Mowitz, Successful Farming magazine has become a leader in the entire area of tractor restoration. Briefly, a few years ago the magazine started a series called Ageless Iron, a supplement to its usual stories about the nuts and bolts of agri-business. The articles have been published twice a year for several years now and are the core of the available information about tractor restoration. Successful Farming has bound all the articles in a single, slim volume, but it is only available as an inducement for subscribing. I can't help but think the articles will eventually be available as a bound, market volume; they're too valuable not to be. In the meantime, you might write Successful Farming, asking about the availability of the articles, ask friends who are subscribers and may have back copies, or dig through your own back copies. Frankly, this is one of the best bodies of information on our hobby there is.

I am reluctant to recommend something I haven't had a chance to take a look at myself, but in this case, since Dave Mowitz and Successful Farming have listed the following, I have more than passing confidence in them. They're worth a try when you're up a tree, right? The thing to do is get hold of Successful Farming's full series, because there you will find not only these few addresses for publications, but other listings for restoration services, decals, tires, lots of other things that are not within the focus of this book but which are darned useful for anyone in tractor repair and restoration. Here again, Dave Mowitz and Successful Farming deserve the gratitude of every rust-blooded American boy!

The 9N-2N-8N-NAA Newsletter
154 Blackwood Ln
Stamford, CT 06903
203/322-7283
    Ford shop manuals for the named models.

Bershire Implement Co. Inc.
Royal Center, IN 46978
219/643-3115
    IHC manuals and literature

Broken Kettle Books
702 East Madison
Fairfield, IA 52556

Robert Campbell
RR 1 Box 348
Newberry, MI 49868

Connecticut Yankee Tractor
Ed Bezanson
85-A Dayton Rd
Waterford, CT 06385
203/442-5182

Jerry Erickson
RR 1
Lyle, MN 55953
504/325-4745, 515/582-4623
    Rumley literature

Marvin Estlow
277 So Stringtown Rd
Quincy, MI 49082
517/639-4906
    Reproduction manuals for Hart-Parr models 12-24, 18-36, and 28-50

Clarence Goodburn
RR 2A-P
Madelia, MN 56062
507/642-3281, 507/642-8481

GRATCO
Tom Franklin
2384 Deborah Ct
Parker, CO 80134

Mike Hunchak
Box 247
Langham, SASK Canada
SOL 210

King's Books
Box 86
Radnor, OH 43066
614/595-3332

Jack Kreeger
7529 Beford Ave
Omaha, NE 68134
    Deere LI and L manuals

Lancaster's
Box 13636-A
Roseville, MN 55113

Lewis
RR 2 Box 508A
Yarmouth, MA 04096
207/846-3080

Massey Collectors News
Box 529
Denver, IA 50622
319/984-5292, 319/352-5524
    Will copy Massey materials

McMillan's Oliver Collectibles
9176 US St 36
Bradford, OH 45308
513/448-2216

Medina Tractor Sales
6080 Norwalk Rd
Medina, OH 44251
800/589-5995
    Ford-Ferguson 9N repair manuals

Walter Miller
6710 Brooklawn Pkwy
Syracuse, NY 13211
315/432-8282

Glen Minarik
RR 1 Box 129
Howells, NE 68641
    IHC materials

Bud Motry
20201 Arthur Rd
Big Rapids, MI 49307
    Antique engine repair booklet $7

Lee Pedersen
78 Taft Ave
Lynbrook, NY 11563

Mike Popp
2730 Oakhurst Ln
Franksville, WI 53126
    Massey-Harris materials

Rice Equipment
20N Sheridan Rd
Clarion, PA 16214
    IHC materials

Larry Rusch
PO Box 698
Freeport, IL 61032
    IHC materials

John Skarstad
Dept of Special Collections
Shields Library
Uni of California
Davis, CA 95616
916/752-1621
   Large collection of shop parts
manuals, copies available at moderate
cost.

Index ◆